UNITED STATES CRYPTOLOGIC HISTORY

Series IV
World War II
Volume 11

Cryptologic Aspects
of
German Intelligence Activities
in South America
during World War II

David P. Mowry

Center for Cryptologic History
National Security Agency
2011

EDITOR'S NOTE: THIS PUBLICATION JOINS TWO CRYPTOLOGIC HISTORY
MONOGRAPHS THAT WERE PUBLISHED SEPARATELY IN 1989.

Cover Photos:
1) The headquarters of the Reich Security Administration's foreign intelligence operations (Department VI), Berlin
2) The ENIGMA served as the standard cipher machine for Germany's military, its agents, and its secret police.

PART I–GERMAN CLANDESTINE ACTIVITIES

Table of Contents

FOREWORD

This is the first of a two-part history of German clandestine activities in South America in World War II. In this first volume, the author, Mr. David Mowry, identifies and presents a thorough account of German intelligence organizations engaged in clandestine work in South America, and a well-researched, detailed report of the U.S. response to the perceived threat. This perception was, as Mr. Mowry alludes to in his conclusions, far greater than any actual danger.

Mr. Mowry's conclusions, in general, are somewhat understated. It seems fairly clear from the evidence that the Germans never expected a great deal from their agents in South America or even in the United States in World War II. The lack of German espionage activity in these areas in WWII stands in stark contrast to the bombings and other activities which occurred during WWI. Perhaps these WWI experiences influenced U.S. policy makers to the extent that they overestimated the danger in WWII. In fact, it might be suggested that South America and the United States were not the major threats of German clandestine activity in WW II, but that Europe, England, North Africa, and the Middle East offered far more potential for beneficial results. An examination of clandestine activities in these areas might produce different conclusions. One might also comment on the extraordinary activity that took place between and among U.S. intelligence organizations in the face of so small and unsuccessful a German effort. In addition to concluding that it had little effect on the outcome of the war, one might also have noted the similarities characterizing the nature of the relationships. Specifically, this includes the relationships in the broader COMINT field during and after the war.

Part two of this history deals with the cryptographic systems used by the various German intelligence organizations engaged in clandestine activities. It is a much more technically oriented work than this volume and an excellent companion piece.

Henry F. Schorreck
NSA Historian
[1989]

Chapter 1

The German Intelligence Services

Perspective

The fall of the Batista government in Cuba in 1959 and the subsequent rise of Castro's Cuba as a Soviet ally in the Western Hemisphere marked the beginning of Russian success in obtaining a foothold in an area that had been the exclusive sphere of influence of the United States.

The concept of carving out a piece of the Western Hemisphere did not originate with the Soviet Union. Since 1823, the year the Monroe Doctrine was enunciated, most of the major European powers tried at one time or another to subvert it. Germany tried twice. The first time, in 1917, Germany planned to attack the United States through Mexico. This plan was foiled by Britain when it provided the United States with a decrypted copy of the famous Zimmermann Telegram. Germany's second attempt was more complex, but in the end, just as unsuccessful.[1]

By 1939, large groups of German nationals had settled in the various countries of Latin America, particularly Argentina, Brazil, and Chile. Germany maintained close contact with these expatriates through commerce, German diplomatic representatives, and pro-Nazi social organizations. German commercial interests in Latin America depended to a large extent on trade with Germany, and various business organizations were brought into the National Socialist fold by appeals to patriotism and by threats of interruption of trade. This large pro-German, if not necessarily pro-Nazi, expatriate community provided a fertile ground for the planting of espionage organizations by the German intelligence services–the Abwehr and, later on, the Reich Security Administration. These two organizations, separately and in combination, were responsible for Germany's espionage operations

before and during World War II. Latin America was probably their major theater of operations, but similar espionage organizations were established all over the world–organizations that would be the objects of considerable scrutiny by Allied intelligence and counterintelligence agencies.[2]

The Abwehr

After the demobilization of the German Army at the end of World War I, the Intelligence office of the General Staff, or IIIb, became an intelligence group attached to the Foreign Armies Branch of the General Staff. Later, with the signing of the Treaty of Versailles, the General Staff itself became the Troops Department, and the Foreign Armies Branch became the Third Branch, or T3, of the Troops Department. The Intelligence Group became the Abwehr Group of T3. The name "Abwehr" (literally, "defense") was the covername given to the counterintelligence group in order to disguise its espionage functions.[3]

On 1 April 1928. the Abwehr Group and the German Navy's espionage unit were combined as the Abwehr Branch, directly subordinate to the Ministry of Defense. In March 1929 this branch was combined with several other offices into a Minister's Department, which later became the High Command of the Armed Forces (OKW). Thus the Abwehr became the military espionage agency it was to be in World War II.[4]

After the Nazi Party came to power, there was considerable friction between the Abwehr and the agencies of the Party, in particular the Security Service (SO). On 1 January 1935 German Navy captain Wilhelm Franz Canaris became the head of the Abwehr and instituted a policy of cooperation which was reciprocated by Reinhardt Heydrich, the head of the SO. This resulted, in December 1936, in an official agreement on division of effort known as the "Ten Commandments," signed by both Canaris and Heydrich, which defined espionage abroad as an Abwehr responsibility.[5]

Admiral Wilhelm Franz Canaris commanded the Abwehr from 1935 to 1944, when his espionage functions were transferred to the Reich Security Administration.

When Canaris assumed command, the Abwehr consisted of six groups: (I) Army Espionage; (II) the Cipher Center; (III) Counterespionage; (IV) Sabotage and Uprisings; (V) Naval Espionage, with liaison with the Navy's intercept service; and (VI) Air Force Espionage. Canaris made the Abwehr an agency concerned purely with espionage by removing the Cipher Center from its jurisdiction. In the years 1936-1938, the service espionage groups were combined as Abwehr I, Military Espionage; Sabotage and Uprisings became Abwehr II; and Counterespionage became Abwehr III. The Naval Intercept Service was added to the Foreign Branch of OKW, which was transferred to the Abwehr, retaining its branch title. In addition, the Abwehr itself was raised to the level of a division of OKW.[6]

Abwehr I, the largest of the branches, consisted of nine groups: Army East; Army West; Army Technical; Marine; Air Force; Technical/Air Force; Economic; Secret (document forgery and espionage paraphernalia); and Communications. Abwehr headquarters in Berlin delegated its functions extensively to AAA posts in other cities, and as it took up any job or entered a new geographical area, it expanded by creating new geographi-

cal subdivisions. Principal posts of the Abwehr in important cities were called Abwehr Posts (Ast). In the Reich there was one Ast to each Military District headquarters.

Known Asts in the Reich, designated by Roman numerals, were as shown in the chart below.

I	Koenigsberg	X	Hamburg
II	Stettin	XI	Hanover
III	Berlin	XII	Wiesbaden
IV	Dresden	XIII	Nuremberg
V	Stuttgart	XIV TO XVI	(probably did not exist)
VI	Muenster	XVII	Vienna
VII	Munich	XVIII	Salzburg
VII	Breslau	XIX	(probably did not exiat)
IX	Kassel	XX	Danzig
		XXI	Posen

Underneath and reporting to the Asts were Branch Posts (abbreviated Nest or Anst, which were located in the less important cities. Subordinate to the Nests were the Message Centers (abbreviated MK), established in small particular Asts inside the Reich. They were given the task of controlling certain enterprises outside the Reich. Thus, the Hamburg Ast was concerned chiefly with naval activity against England and America and was active in South America, in the Iberian Peninsula, and in Greece. Muenster dealt with roads and communications in enemy territory; Dresden specialized in targets for aerial bombing. Stettin handled naval activity against Russia in the Baltic and also Group I left in Norway. Breslau handled action in Czechoslovakia, Wiesbaden in France and Belgium, and Vienna in the Balkans and the Near East. An Ast was designated an Abwehr Control Post (Alst) to take over control of Abwehr operations for specific purposes, as was Wiesbaden in 1940 for the invasion of France.

There were also Abwehr units called Combat Organizations (KO), which were similar to Asts but operated in neutral and unfriendly countries, including Sweden, Finland, Switzerland, Bulgaria, Turkey, Spain, Portugal, and briefly, North Africa.

Personnel of the KO used embassies and legations as cover. The first of these were established in Madrid and Shanghai in 1937 and in the Netherlands in 1938. The KOs were attached to the German embassies and ran agent nets in the respective countries. By May 1942, there were KOs in Portugal, Spain, Switzerland, Sweden, Finland, Bulgaria, Spanish Morocco (Casablanca), Yugoslavia (Zagreb), China (Shanghai), and Turkey.[7]

The Reich Security Administration

The Security Service was originally a part of the organization called the General Protection Squad (the infamous Blackshirts or SS). Its mission was to gather intelligence about people hostile to Hitler and the Nazi Party. It was the intelligence organ of the Nazi Party. In June 1936 Himmler was made Reichsfuehrer SS and Chief of the German Police. One of his first acts was the appointment of the first important figure in the history of the Reich Security Administration (RSHA), Reinhard Heydrich, the first chief of the Sicherheitspolizei or Security Police (SiPo) and the SD. Heydrich and Himmler were responsible for combining the security services of the SS and the State Police into the RSHA in 1939. As the head of the RSHA, Heydrich concen-

trated almost entirely on eliminating opposition to the Third Reich. Since the "Ten Commandments" defined espionage abroad as largely the function of the Abwehr, Department VI (Foreign Intelligence) of the RSHA was an insignificant unit before 1942. Although Himmler had given orders that he must have a foreign intelligence service of his own, the RSHA did not have the right kind of personnel for this work; very few of its officers had any knowledge of foreign countries or languages.[8]

The character of the RSHA changed after the assassination of Heydrich in 1942 with the rise to power of two new figures, Ernst Kaltenbrunner and Walter Schellenberg. Kaltenbrunner succeeded Heydrich as head of the RSHA, and Schellenberg became the chief of Department VI in the same year. Continual competition between Department VI and the Abwehr eroded the latter's authority until Schellenberg took over its espionage and sabotage sections in May 1944. At that time, Canaris was demoted to head of a special staff for economic warfare. He was arrested on 23 July 1944 for complicity in the bomb attempt on Hitler and was executed on 8 April 1945.[9]

Reinhard Heydrich headed the Reich Security Administration from its creation in 1939 until his assassination in 1942.

Walter Schellenberg, chief of the Reich Security Administration's Department VI, assumed control of the Abwehr's espionage sections in May 1944.

*The headquarters of the Reich Security Administration's foreign intelligence operations
(Department VI), Berlin*

After taking over the Abwehr, the RSHA was divided into eight departments, only two of which, Department VI (Foreign Intelligence) and Military Intelligence, ran espionage agents in the field. Military Intelligence assumed responsibility for espionage in the frontline combat areas, formerly the responsibility of Abwehr I, while Department VI absorbed the Asts' responsibilities (or espionage in foreign countries. The following was the organization of Department VI as late as January 1945:

This was the opposition. Its story and the story of the Allied organizations involved in counterespionage SIGINT in World War II follow.

Department	Function
Amt VIA	Organization
Amt VIB	West Europe (neutral, allied, and occupied countries)
Amt VIC	Russia, Near East, Far East (including Japan)
Amt VID	Western Hemisphere, Great Britain, Scandinavia
Amt VIE	Southeast Europe (including allied and occupied areas)
Amt VIF	Technical Support
Amt VIG	Scientific-Methodic Research Service
Amt VI Wi/T	Economics and Technology
Amt VIS	Sabotage
Amt VI Kult	Nonscientific Domestic Acquisition Service
Amt VIZ	Military Counterespionage and Personnel Checks
Abwehr	Civilian Counterespionage and Personnel Checks[10]

Chapter 2

Axis Agent Operations in Latin America

In his report on his trip to England in 1943, Colonel Alfred McCormack stated that the Coast Guard had abdicated to the British Government Code & Cipher School (GC&CS) its responsibility for all clandestine communications other than those concerning the Western Hemisphere. While McCormack was certainly overstating the case, with equal certainty the Coast Guard's primary interest was in agent communications between Germany and Latin America. These communications were primarily the responsibility of Operation BOLIVAR,11 the code name for an espionage project carried out by Department VID4 of the SD. It was active in Brazil, Paraguay, and Argentina, with ramifications reaching into the official circles of those countries.[12]

SARGO

Johannes Siegfried Becker (SARGO) was the main figure in the project and the person responsible for most of the organizing of espionage operations in South America. Becker was first sent to Buenos Aires by the SD in May 1940. His original mission, and that of Heinz Lange (JANSEN), who followed him shortly after, was sabotage. In August, because of protests by the German embassy, this was revised to one of espionage only. Becker and Lange were soon identified by the authorities as agents, and in September 1940

Johannes Siegfried Becker (SARGO)

moved to Brazil where Becker made contact with Gustav Albrecht Engels.

Gustav Albrecht Engels (ALFREDO) had originally been recruited by Jobst Raven of Abwehr IW in 1939 to provide economic intelligence on the Western Hemisphere to the Abwehr. He had established an economic espionage organization, reporting to Germany via the radio transmitter owned by his company, the Allgemeine Elektrizitaets Gesellschaft (General Electric Company), headquartered in Krefeld. Becker transformed Engels's organization into an espionage organization reporting on all subjects of interest to German intelligence. By mid-1941, Engels's radio station, CEL, which was located in Sao Paulo, Brazil, was functioning smoothly with agents in both Brazil and the United States. It provided information on shipping, economic and industrial affairs, war production, and military movements in the United States, and political and military developments in Brazil. One of the agents in the United States who frequently came to Brazil to talk to Engels was Dusko Popov (IVAN), known to the British as TRICYCLE—one of the most successful double agents of World War II.[13]

Operation BOLIVAR agents included the naval and air attaché in Chile, Ludwig von Bohlen (BACH); the naval attaché in Rio de Janeiro, Hermann Bohny (UNCLE ERNEST); the military attaché in Buenos Aires and Rio de Janeiro, General Niedefuhr; and the naval attaché in Buenos Aires, Captain Dietrich Niebuhr (DIEGO), who headed the espionage organization in Argentina. In mid-1941 Herbert von Heyer (HUMBERTO) joined the organization, providing maritime intelligence.[14]

The Brazilian Nets

Engels's organization was not the only one operating in Brazil. Three other clandestine radio stations, each serving a different spy net, had started operating in 1941. Radio station LIR, in Rio de Janeiro, had started communications with MAX, in Germany, in May. The LIRMAX group operated in Brazil, Argentina, Uruguay, and Ecuador and was centered on a commercial information service, the Informadora Rapida Limitada (RITA), run by Heribert O. J. Muller (PRINZ). The radio station was run by Friedrich Kempter (KOENIG). Von Heyer, HUMBERTO in the CELALD organization, was VESTA in the LIRMAX group. There were other overlaps in personnel, with the two groups cooperating extensively. Von Heyer was an employee of the Theodor Wille Company, several of whose employees were involved in another net centered on station CIT in Recife, Brazil. The CIT net began operation in June 1941 and was located entirely in Brazil. A third group, consisting of only two agents, Fritz Noak and Herbert Winterstein, was located between Santos and Rio de Janeiro and communicated with LFS in Germany from September 1941 to January 1942. It was not connected with the CELALD-LIRMAX-CIT group.[15]

Regrouping

At the end of November 1941, Becker had returned to Germany for a conference with his superiors and was thus out of harm's way when Brazilian police rounded up enemy agents on 18 March 1942. During this conference it was decided that Becker would be in charge of South American operations (all of which were to be connected by radio) with Buenos Aires acting as the control station for the net and reporting directly to Berlin. Lange was to organize an espionage net in Chile, and Johnny Hartmuth (GUAPO), a Department VID 2 agent who had elected to remain in South America, would organize a net in Paraguay. An agent named Franczok (LUNA) would control the radio network which was to be established. Lange,

Hartmuth, and Franczok were all in Paraguay, having fled from Brazil in March.[16]

In February 1943, after considerable difficulty, Becker managed to return to Buenos Aires as a stowaway on a ship traveling from Spain to Argentina. Lange, Hartmuth, and Franczok had managed to airmail one transmitter to Paraguay before they left Brazil and, setting up a temporary headquarters near Asunción, had reestablished contact with Berlin. Upon Becker's orders, this station was transferred to Buenos Aires in May, leaving Hartmuth in Paraguay. Lange proceeded to Chile.

Once the transfer to Buenos Aires had taken place, Becker and Franczok immediately began establishing the planned radio network. Becker wanted to establish a transmitter in every South American republic, but was successful only in Paraguay, Chile, and Argentina, where he was at this time establishing an espionage organization.[17]

The Chilean Nets

When Lange went to Chile, there was already an agent organization and radio station in operation and Lange fitted himself into it as an independent operator with his own sources. The station, using callsign PYL to communicate with REW in Germany, had been established in April or May 1941, apparently by Ludwig von Bohlen and Friedrich von Schulz Hausman (CASERO). By February 1942, reports were being passed from agents in Chile, Peru, Colombia, Ecuador, Guatemala, Mexico, and the United States. The major figures in the organization were von Bohlen in Santiago; Bruno Dittman (DINTERIN), the actual head of the net, in Valparaiso; Friedrich von Schulz Hausman, who had relocated to Buenos Aires; and George Nicolaus (MAX) in Mexico.[18]

The PYLREW net's tie with Project BOLIVAR was revealed through intercept, particularly in July 1941, when von Bohlen was instructed by radio to contact von Heyer in Rio de Janeiro to obtain a supply of secret inks and developers which von Bohlen had ordered from Germany.

The PYLREW organization was centered on the Compania Transportes Maritimos (COTRAS), formerly a branch of Norddeutscher Lloyd. Von Schulz Hausman had been the manager of the Norddeutscher Lloyd Shipping Agency in Chile before moving to Argentina, and had been succeeded in that job by Dittman. Other PYLREW personnel who had been associated with Norddeutscher Lloyd were Hans Blume (FLOR), a radio technician at PYL, and Heinrich Reiners (TOM), who had worked for Norddeutscher Lloyd in Panama before opening a maritime freight office in Valparaiso. Reiners's sister was married to Blume, and Reiners's wife was the drop for the agents of the net.[19]

Operation JOLLE

The first traffic passed from Buenos Aires concerned finances, the organization of the South American net, Argentine politics, and the establishment of a courier system between Argentina and Spain using crewmen aboard Spanish merchant vessels. Once the network got into full operation, traffic volume increased to as much as fifteen messages a day. In January 1944, the Argentine government arrested a number of German and Spanish espionage agents, and Becker and Franczok were forced into hiding. Communications were interrupted for about a month and never again resumed the former level. When communications were reestablished, Becker asked Berlin for radio equipment, money, and secret ink materials. This request resulted in Operation JOLLE.[20]

It had become increasingly difficult to keep the agent organizations in South America supplied with funds and cryptomaterial. As with Comintern agents between the wars, a primary method of financing agent operations was through the smuggling of precious gems which could then be sold to obtain operating funds. To this the Germans added the smuggling of expensive pharmaceuticals which could readily be sold on the black market.

The gems and the pharmaceuticals could be transmitted via couriers ("wolves") who travelled as crewmen aboard Spanish ships. This was not, however, a satisfactory method for transporting crypto-equipment and keying materials, for moving agents in and out of target countries, or for shipping bulky reports back to Germany. Up to that time, the normal method used by Department VI to introduce agents into neutral or hostile countries had been to land them from submarines. This had not been particularly successful and, with increasing Allied dominance of the sea, was becoming an even more problematical method of transport. Likewise, the courier system was in danger because of Spanish awareness that Germany was losing the war. It was as a result of these circumstances, and of the difficulty of evading Allied patrols in the Atlantic that operations such as MERCATOR and JOLLE were conceived.[21]

Kurt Gross, the Chief of Department VI D4, had been looking for other methods, and Becker's request gave him an opening. He decided to send not only supplies and money, but also personnel. Two men were to be sent to Argentina initially. Hansen (COBIJA) was a trained radio operator who spoke fluent Spanish, having lived in South America for twenty years. Schroell (VALIENTE), a native of Luxembourg, was a sailor by profession and spoke English; he also had had some radio experience. The mission, as planned, involved the two agents being transported to Argentina, where they would eventually separate from Becker and make their way northward. Ultimately, Hansen was supposed to settle in Mexico and Schroell in the United States, obtaining a position in a war plant there. Hansen was instructed to set up a radio transmitter in Mexico and send in reports of information both he and Schroell had obtained concerning the United States. The two were to maintain a channel of communication. Further, they were to recruit new agents and establish an espionage net covering Central America and the United States.

In preparation for their mission, Hansen and Schroell were given a course of training which included the use of secret inks, ciphers, and the microdot camera. They were also given suicide pills, two each, for use in an emergency. False identification papers were provided by Department VIF. They were given no persons to contact other than Becker, either in North or South America, since Department VID had no one there who could assist the project. They were also not given any cover addresses for use in establishing communications with Germany, as it was assumed that they would be successful in their radio endeavors. As a supplementary method of transmitting information, they were instructed to develop a courier system which could be coordinated with the organization in Spain run by Karl Arnold (THEO or ARNOLD). In using couriers, it was planned that they would use both secret writing and microdots.

Although Gross had given them the broad goals of their mission, he emphasized that they would be expected to use their own initiative to a great extent and capitalize on any opportunity which presented itself to make the project more effective. How they were to proceed from Argentina, up through South America to Mexico and the United States, would be up to them. It was expected, however, that Becker would be able to help them in getting started.[22]

Allied intelligence, reading the exchanges between Berlin and Buenos Aires, was convinced that a submarine was to be used for the transfer and that the German term "Jolle" (English "yawl") was simply a cover term. It appeared from his messages that Becker thought the same, but on 30 March 1944, Berlin told Argentina that the vessel to be used was "not a yawl, but a cutter," and that planning was continuing. This was the first specific indication that a submarine was not to be involved.[23]

MERCATOR I and MERCATOR II

In fact, the Abwehr had used a small sailing boat in August 1942 to land agents in Southwest Africa and again, in May-June 1943, to land agents in Brazil. The vessel used was a thirty-six-ton ketch

named *Passim*. On her first voyage, codenamed MERCATOR I, *Passim* had sailed from Brest to Southwest Africa carrying three agents. Two of them had been landed north of Hollams Bird Island, and the third near Sao Paulo de Loanda. She then returned to Bayonne after 142 days at sea and was sent on to Arcachon for repairs.[24]

On her second voyage, codenamed MERCATOR II, *Passim* sailed from Arcachon on 9 June 1943 and delivered two agents, Wilhelm Koepff (HEDWIG) and William Baarn, to Brazil. Wilhelm Heinrich Koepff was a German small businessman who had settled in Peru after World War I, in which he had served in the infantry. He was an ardent Nazi, and his reputation as a Nazi activist resulted in his firm being blacklisted by the British and the Americans in 1941. This had a disastrous effect on his finances, and he took to drink. When the countries of the Western Hemisphere broke off relations with Germany in 1942, he arranged to have himself repatriated and in Germany he volunteered for service in the Abwehr as an espionage agent. After intensive training he reported aboard *Passim* on 15 May 1943 to meet his partner, William Marcus Baarn. Baarn was a black from Dutch Guiana with a reputation as a troublemaker. During the thirties he had worked as a merchant seaman in American waters and then went to Amsterdam as a stowaway on a Dutch ship. He had worked at various jobs in Holland and for some reason had made no attempt to get out when Germany invaded the Low Countries. He was recruited by the Abwehr, whom he was in no position to refuse, and trained in radio operation and cryptography for four months.[25]

Passim sailed from Arcachon on 23 May 1943. The two agents were put ashore on Gargahu Beach, near Sao Joao da Barra, Brazil, on the night of 9/10 August 1943. Despite the high hopes of the Abwehr, both men surrendered to Brazilian police within twenty-four hours. The Brazilian authorities "turned" Koepff and used him as a controlled agent until March 1944. He and Baarn were tried in March 1945 and sentenced to twenty-five years in prison.[26]

The Planning for Operation JOLLE

Gross had determined that *Passim* was still in Arcachon and that naval captain Heinz Garbers, who had commanded her on her first two voyages, was available. Garbers was a well-known sportsman who had crossed the Atlantic in a sailboat in 1938. The justification for using a vessel such as *Passim* was that although slower than submarines or merchant vessels, a regular route could be established and such a boat could easily be mistaken for a Portuguese, Spanish, or South American fishing lugger, and thus be ignored by Allied patrol vessels. Arrangements were made, and Hansen and Schroell sailed aboard *Passim* on 27 April 1944 with quite a large cargo, the bulk of which consisted of items sent for resale. Siemens, Telefunken, Merck Chemical, and a pharmaceutical company (probably Bayer) had sent orders through Franczok for radio and other electrical equipment, as well as for chemical and medical supplies. In this way, these companies would be aided and the money received from them would contribute considerably to the finances of the spy ring. The latter purpose was also served by the shipment of a stock of needles used in the weaving or mending of silk stockings to be resold by the agency. Berlin also sent along plans for a device to make wood gas generators.

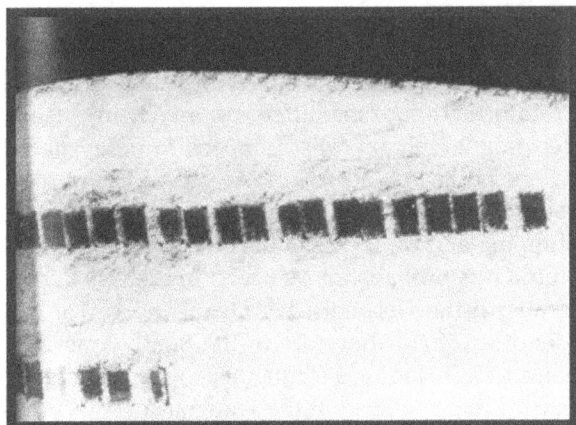

Microdots taped inside the label of an envelope sent by German agents in Mexico to Lisbon

An attempt was to be made to sell a license for the manufacture of these generators.

In all, they took some fifty tons of material with them, including complete radio sets, parts for use by Becker and for the new project, a microdot camera, and a supply of diamonds which had been obtained in Holland. Hansen and Schroell also took with them foreign currency in the form of Argentine pesos, British pounds, and American dollars which totalled some $100,000 in value. This money was to be shared with Becker. It was meant that Hansen and Schroell would remain in the Western Hemisphere indefinitely, and the money given to them was to last over two years.[27]

At this point, the plans for the landing in Argentina were extremely confused. The original plans had been cancelled, and Becker did not understand what Berlin wanted. Finally, three possible landing points had been picked: Necochea, Miramar, and Mar del Plata. Berlin considered Necochea to be the preferable one, particularly since Becker had reported that both sea and coast were unacceptable at Miramar. Becker was insisting on four weeks' advance notice of the landing; three days forewarning from *Passim*; a communications plan for contacting *Passim*; and instructions on loading and unloading.[28]

The communications plan was sent on 6 June. Becker complained on 9 June about the short notice and about the lack of internal serialization on Berlin's messages, which sometimes made it difficult to understand references. As a consequence of the latter, apparently, several of Berlin's messages went unanswered, and Becker was instructed to contact *Passim* on his own and set up a communications plan.[29]

At this point, it would seem that Franczok (who was in charge of communications at the Argentine end) complained about the preparations, or lack thereof, because Berlin responded:

SAVE YOUR CRITICISM FOR YOURSELVES WHEN YOU DO NOT KNOW FULL DETAILS; IT ONLY INDICATES THAT THROUGH YOUR CLEVER CONDUCT THE ORIGIN- ALLY CONTEMPLATED LANDING HAS ALREADY BEEN DISCOVERED. JOLLE HAS RECEIVED YOUR INSTRUCTIONS ON MIRAMAR PREPARATIONS AND WILL, IF POSSIBLE, CARRY THEM OUT. [THE] MATTER WILL BE SETTLED BY RED [BERLIN] CENTER. [30]

Franczok sent communications and landing instructions to *Passim* on 21 June, setting Mogotes as the place and 0200 as the time of day for the landing. Garbers preferred Punta Indio, but Becker would not accept the suggestion, insist- ing on Mogotes. After some further delays, the operation was finally carried out on the night of 30 June/1 July, and *Passim* set sail for Europe, taking Philip Imhoff (BIENE), Heinz Lange, and Juergen Sievers (SANTOS) as passengers.[31]

Shortly after Hansen and Schroell arrived in Argentina, most of the members of Operation BOLIVAR were arrested, breaking up the ring once and for all, and effective espionage activity by Department VID 4 in the Western Hemisphere was ended.[32]

The End of Operation JOLLE

Garbers had intended to put into port at Bordeaux upon *Passim's* return to France, but the Normandy invasion had made that inadvisable. Lange wanted the boat to return to South America and succeeded in convincing some of the crew to agree with him, but Garbers threatened to have him prosecuted for incitement to mutiny and trea- son. Berlin ordered *Passim* to Vigo, Spain, where she docked the night of 17 September, posing as the French ship *St. Barbara*, a name she had carried on her voyage to Brazil in 1943. Garbers, accompa- nied by Lange, went ashore the next day to visit the

German consulate. Garbers returned later, alone and wearing civilian clothes. He had found that Karl Arnold had been advised of their coming and had made some preparations to care for them. For the next three or four days, all the men remained aboard *Passim* with a Spanish police boat along- side. They were then issued passes giving them freedom of movement in Vigo. They were allowed to move to the Hotel Central, but both captain and crew had to report every morning aboard the Spanish cruiser *Navarra,* which was lying in the harbor. When the cruiser sailed, they then reported to the Spanish police each morning.

After a month under loose arrest, the men were released by the Spanish and traveled to Madrid, leaving *Passim* lying at Vigo under Spanish guard. In Madrid they stayed at the German-owned Hotel Aragon for four to six days. From Madrid, Garbers went on to Barcelona, followed by the others, who arrived on 7-8 November. They then left Barcelona by air in groups of two or three. It took ten days for the entire party to reach Berlin. Garbers did attempt to have Lange prosecuted, but Gross arranged for the charges to be dropped.[33]

The Benefits Derived

Commander L. T. Jones, the head of the Coast Guard cryptologic operation, wrote an evalua- tion of the Allied SIGINT effort against BOLIVAR in 1944. He pointed out that, basically, the type of information transmitted by an enemy agent depends largely on what happens to be available where he is located. BOLIVAR agents were able to provide reports on the movements of merchant shipping and on local political developments. The traffic was probably more useful to the Allies than it was to the Germans, because it did reveal the identities of collaborators in the South American countries, including a former Argentine minister of marine and the head of the Paraguayan Air Force. The Allies also were able to obtain from clandestine traffic the details of planning for the 20 December 1943 revolution in Bolivia and another in Chile which was nipped in the bud. Both of these were backed by Germans working through the Argentine government.

In addition, the intercept of clandestine traffic allowed the Allies to maintain continuity on the agents operating in the Western Hemisphere. This information led to a number of arrests, the most celebrated at the time being that of Osmar Alberto Hellmuth on 4 November 1943.[34]

An Argentine naval officer, Hellmuth, unbeknownst to Argentina, was a German collaborator. His control, Hans Harnisch (BOSS), claimed to be the personal representative of Heinrich Himmler and had extensive contacts in the highest reaches of the Argentine government. As a result of negotiations between Harnisch and various Argentine officials, including President Ramirez and various cabinet ministers, Hellmuth was appointed Argentine consul in Barcelona. This appointment served to cover his actual mission: to proceed to Germany to ensure that country that Argentina had no intention of severing relations with her. He was also to confer with the SD and other German officials on matters of mutual interest and was to obtain German permission for the return to Argentina from Sweden of the Argentine tanker *Buenos Aires*, carrying a load of German-supplied arms.[35]

Most of the details of this planning were known to the Allies through BOLIVAR traffic. As a consequence, when the *Cabo de Hornos*, aboard which Hellmuth was traveling to Spain, made a routine stop at Trinidad, British authorities removed him from the ship and placed him under arrest. Argentina made a formal protest to Britain. When the ramifications of the affair were learned, however, there was a change in position. The Argentine minister of foreign affairs instructed his ambassador in London on 17 December to inform Great Britain that Hellmuth's appointment had been cancelled and that if the British would release Hellmuth, his letters patent would also be cancelled and the British could then do with him as they saw fit.[36]

In early 1946, when the State Department was preparing a case against the Peronista government of Argentina regarding its wartime support of the Axis, it requested permission to use clandestine intercept as part of its evidence. Although the Navy refused to give blanket approval for such usage, an accommodation was reached, and information from clandestine communications was fused with information from other sources in preparing the indictment. This was Operation BOLIVAR's final contribution to the Allied war effort.[37]

Chapter 3

Allied Operations Concerned with the Clandestine Problem

U.S. Navy (1917-1941)

During World War I, the U.S. Navy had built up an integrated organization (the Code and Signal Section of the Office of Naval Communications) for the compilation, production, distribution, and accounting of codes and ciphers. This section, also known as OP-58, was established as a part of the Division of Operations sometime between 2 January and 1 April 1917. Its first head was Lieutenant Russell Willson (USN), who was ordered to Washington, D.C., on the former date. The Confidential Publications Section (as the Code and Signal Section was called before October 1917) had originally been intended to centralize the Navy's storage, accounting, and distribution of confidential publications, while the Bureau of Navigation (BUNAV) was responsible for the preparation of codes and ciphers. BUNAV's Signal Office had published the *Telegraphic Dictionaries* since at least 1848 and the Navy *General Signal Books* since the Civil War. By 1894 the dictionaries and the signal books had been combined, and in 1913 there was a section in the *General Signal Book* providing five-letter code groups that were used for secret communications until the Navy "A-Code" was constructed by the Code and Signal Section.[38]

By 1 December 1917, the OIC of the Code and Signal Section, Lieutenant Commander Milo F. Draemel, had been made Assistant to the Director of Naval Communications (DNC) for Codes and Signals. The section had been made a part of the Naval Communication Service, but since it was not performing a staff function, it was not part of the Director's office. The section was redesignated OP-18 on or about January 1920 but remained in the same command status until July 1922, when it became OP-20-G.[39]

The Registered Publications Section was created on 31 March 1923 to standardize and centralize the issuance of and accounting for classified publications. As originally conceived in May 1921, this section was to be a part of OP-20-G, but there is no record of its OP-number until 1 July 1926, when it was listed as OP-20-P, with Lieutenant E. K. Jett, later Chief Engineer of the Federal Communications Commission (FCC), as OIC.[40]

In January 1924 Lieutenant Laurance F. Safford was ordered to OP-20-G to take over the newly established Research Desk in that section. "Research Desk" was the covername for the newly formed communications intelligence activity. This marked the entry of the Navy into communications intelligence, aside from an interim effort begun by the Office of Naval Intelligence (ONI) in 1917, when a Cipher Room was established to decrypt enemy messages. The Cipher Room was absorbed by the War Department's Bureau of Military Intelligence in 1918. The initial staff or the Research Desk consisted of Lieutenant Safford and four civilians, later supplemented by two enlisted radiomen.[41]

According to U.S. Navy captain Joseph N. Wenger, there were two factors that governed the placing of communications intelligence activities in the Office of Naval Communications (ONC) rather than in ONI. First of all, the Director of Naval Communications (DNC) showed interest and initiative in getting them placed under his jurisdiction. Secondly, over a period of time, the cognizant naval authorities recognized that this was the proper location, as they realized that the highly technical business of intercept and direction finding would be most effectively and economically operated in conjunction with other technical activities. The collection and production of SIGINT involved the same skills, training, equipment, and techniques as communications, and thus belonged in that branch of the Navy. In addition, from both a security and a budgetary viewpoint, it made sense to collocate SIGINT sites with communications stations.

Eventually OP-20-G would have control over communications intelligence, communications security, and registered publications. The Registered Publications Section continued to carry the designation OP-20-P, but by 1932 it was included as a subunit of the Code and Signal Section. Letters were assigned to the subordinate desks by 1926, the year in which Lieutenant Safford was relieved by Lieutenant Joseph J. Rochefort as head of the Research Desk. In June 1932 OP-20-G consisted of the OIC and his office staff; OP-20-P, Registered Publications; OP-20-GC, the Codes and Ciphers Desk; OP-20-GS, the Visual Signals Desk; and OP-20-GX, the Research Desk.[42]

The Research Desk was renamed the Research and Radio Intelligence Desk in 1933. In June 1934 these functions were split between two desks: the Research Desk, OP-20-GY, and the Radio Intercept Desk, OP-20-GX; and OP-20-P was removed from OP-20-G cognizance and supervision. A new section, the Language Section, was created in October 1934, with the designation OP-20-GZ. On 11 March 1935, OP-20-G was reorganized to consist of the Cryptographic Section (GC), headed by Lieutenant Chester C. Wood; the Security Section (GS), headed by Lieutenant Lee W. Parke; the Intercept and Tracking Section (GX), headed by Lieutenant Commander John S. Harper; the Cryptanalytic Section (GY), headed by Lieutenant Commander Joseph N. Wenger; and the Translation Section (GZ), headed by Lieutenant Commander Thomas B. Birtley, Jr. In this reorganization, OP-20-G was renamed the Communications Security Group, with Lieutenant Commander Laurance F. Safford in command after March 1936.[43]

In the early days the Navy's SIGINT activity in Washington was so small that no formal organization other than that mentioned above was necessary. However, with the beginning of Navy

success against the Japanese naval ciphers in the early 1930s and the production of operational intelligence on Japanese naval maneuvers, it became obvious that expansion was necessary to exploit the possibilities that had appeared. Even so, in 1936 the total strength of the Communications Security Group was only eleven officers, eighty-eight enlisted men, and fifteen civilians, a total of 147. Lieutenant Joseph N. Wenger's 1937 planning study, "Military Study–Communications Intelligence Research Activities," was the first serious attempt at defining the course to be pursued. The organization conceptualized by this paper consisted of a main analysis, administration, and coordinating center in Washington, D.C., with subordinate area analysis centers, advance processing units at intercept sites, and mobile units for close support of major operating commanders. The study also defined the need for fast and secure communications within the naval organization and for liaison with the Army and the Coast Guard. All of these ideas would eventually be implemented.[44]

OP-20-G underwent two more renamings before the beginning of World War II. On 15 March 1939 it became the Radio Intelligence Section of the Office of Naval Communications, and on 1 October 1939 it became the Communications Security Section. The Cryptanalytic Section was relieved of its responsibility for training and research in 1939, and these functions were combined in the Research and Training Section, OP-20-GR. By January 1941 OP-20-G consisted of some sixty persons plus a few small field activities. On 7 December 1941 the strength was 75 officers, 645 enlisted men, and 10 civilians: a total of 730. It continued to be headed by Commander Safford, who, at his own request, was redesignated from "General Line" to "Engineering (i.e., cryptographic) Duty Only" on 12 September 1941. He was promoted to captain on 1 December 1941.[45]

The U.S. Coast Guard (1931-1941)

The Coast Guard Communications Intelligence Section was established in 1931 to solve the illicit shortwave radio traffic exchanged between groups of smugglers and other criminals violating the laws enforced by the six enforcement bureaus of the Treasury Department. Through the monitoring of illegal radio networks during the time when smuggling was at its height, Coast Guard intercept operators developed a specialized technique which proved most effective in identifying and following illicit stations.[46]

Until late 1935 eighty percent of the work done by the Cryptanalytic Unit had been cryptanalytic. After October of that year, there was a heavy increase in cryptographic duties when the secretary of the treasury tasked the unit with creating a Treasury Department cryptosystem. At that time, he also tasked the unit with cooperating with the Bureau of Customs and Narcotics to suppress the smuggling of illegal drugs into the United States and with certain responsibilities in the field of foreign exchange.[47]

As a result of these tasks, the end of prohibition did not reduce to any appreciable degree the duties of the Intelligence Division. The division remained the assembly and distribution agent for information of every kind pertaining to the phases of law enforcement with which the entire Treasury Department was charged and in which State, Justice, Commerce, and other departments of the government were interested. In spite of this, its strength decreased by a third between March 1936 and March 1937 because of budget restrictions brought on by the Depression. In 1937 only the five persons listed below were left.

Mrs. Elizebeth S. Friedman, P-4, Cryptanalyst in Charge
Mr. Vernon E. Cooley, P-2, Assistant Cryptanalyst
Mr. Robert E. Gordon, P-2, Assistant Cryptanalyst
Mr. Robert J. Fenn, P-1, Junior Cryptanalyst
Mr. Charles H. Withers, CAF-3. Cryptographic Clerk

According to Lieutenant Frank E. Pollio, the acting chief of the Intelligence Division at the time, similar organizations in the Army and Navy were composed of twelve to twenty-five persons and

were considered a necessary adjunct to national security. In the Treasury Department, cryptanalytic personnel were necessary both for military security as it pertained to the Coast Guard and for law enforcement as it pertained to the department. The strength of five was maintained through 1940. At the end of that year, two billets were added to bring the strength up to seven: four professional grade cryptanalysts, one IBM operator, and two typists.[48]

After the establishment of the Money Stabilization Board under the Treasury Department, the Cryptanalytic Unit provided this Board with information in connection with foreign exchange control; and after 1938 it maintained a close watch for any clues in radio traffic pointing to sudden changes in the international situation. In August 1939 the unit was transferred to the Communications Division of the Coast Guard, where it operated in response to requests from the Intelligence Division and other Treasury bureaus.[49]

Organized smuggling had practically disappeared by 1939, and for several months before the German invasion of Poland, the Coast Guard had been given assignments monitoring the shipborne communications of potential belligerents and watching for, among other things, indications of possible entry into a war by other nations. This was done to forewarn Treasury, which could then take appropriate actions concerning the freezing of funds.[50]

With the outbreak of war in Europe, the Treasury Department's statutory responsibility for enforcement of U.S. neutrality brought on a number of new responsibilities for the Coast Guard. Among these were the sealing of communications equipment on all belligerent vessels entering U.S. ports and the prevention of nonneutral communications concerning shipping or the movement of belligerent ships.

In monitoring communications pursuant to this latter responsibility, USCG monitoring stations reported late in 1940 that they were intercepting traffic similar to that of the old rumrunner transmissions. When these messages were solved, they proved to contain military information from somewhere in England (apparently the transmissions of agent SNOW, see following), These solutions were sent to ONI, G-2, State Department, and the FBI; and work was continued on additional related circuits which were found while monitoring the first one. Intercept and analysis of these communications were to constitute a major part of the Coast Guard's contribution to intelligence during World War II.[51]

In late 1940, Lieutenant Commander Pollio, by then Intelligence Officer of the Coast Guard, and Lieutenant L.T. Jones, who as a lieutenant commander and then commander, would be in charge of the wartime Cryptanalytic Unit, had submitted their recommendations for improving the communications and intelligence postures of the Coast Guard. Among other things, they had recommended the establishment of permanent radio intercept stations in the New York, Jacksonville, New Orleans, San Francisco, and Honolulu Districts. These stations would be organized along the lines of regular Coast Guard radio stations but for technical reasons would be kept totally separate from regular communications stations. Pollio and Jones also recommended that the officers in charge of these stations have a knowledge of cryptanalysis. The stations would copy traffic from known illicit stations and search for new ones. By having officers qualified in cryptanalysis in charge, it was expected that there would be little difficulty in distinguishing illicit transmissions from other traffic of no interest.[52]

The Coast Guard (and the Navy) considered the term "clandestine radio intelligence" to include transmissions from all stations operating on radio nets which handled communications for enemy agents. Often these nets included stations within Axis or Axis-occupied territory, where they were certainly not clandestine. For the most part, these nets passed Abwehr and SD traffic, but they also sometimes passed diplomatic or even military communications. However, agent traffic could be, and often was, passed over commercial or diplomatic facilities. As a consequence, Commander L.T. Jones considered the cryptosystem used to be the only valid standard for discrimination.[53]

On 26 June 1939, a memorandum from President Franklin D. Roosevelt to the members of his cabinet ordered the investigation of all espionage, counterespionage, and sabotage matters centralized in ONI, the Military Intelligence Division (MID) of the War Department, and the FBI. On that date all government agencies other than the Army and Navy intelligence organizations had been ordered to turn over to the FBI all "data, information, or material bearing directly or indirectly on espionage, counterespionage, or sabotage." Since the Coast Guard was a Treasury agency until late 1941, all clandestine material intercepted was thus forwarded to the FBI. In January 1941 the FBI began requesting Coast Guard assistance in the solution of this traffic. In the spring of the same year, the Coast Guard asked for and received permission from the secretary of the treasury to distribute information to the Treasury Department, State Department, ONI, and Army Intelligence in addition to the FBI. It thus developed more or less by a sequence of events rather than by any definite plan that the Coast Guard worked more closely with ONI than with ONC from June 1941 to February 1942.[54]

During 1940 and 1941, the Coast Guard also received miscellaneous intercepted traffic from the Federal Communications Commission (FCC). The FCC, in addition to performing its statutory regulatory duties, began in 1940 to be active in providing the armed forces with copies of the traffic of "suspect" transmitters. In late July of that year, Commander J. F. Farley, the Communications Officer of the Coast Guard, requested FCC monitoring of certain unidentified transmitters operating on the high frequency band; those using callsigns with the pattern "1TLE," "2TLE," etc., and possibly sending five-letter encrypted traffic. The tasking was implemented, and in October Farley expressed the Coast Guard's appreciation and requested that the assignment be continued.[55]

The Federal Communications Commission (1911-1941)

The earliest known attempts by the United States to monitor radio communications had their inception in 1911. Under the Radio Act of 24 June 1910, radio jurisdiction was placed in the Department of Commerce and Labor, and a Radio Service was organized in that department on 1 July 1911. When the department was split in 1913, supervision of the provisions of the Radio Acts of 1910 and 1912 went to the Department of Commerce. The duties of the Radio Division included inspecting radio stations, examining radio operators, determining the power of radio stations, and conducting investigations of interstation interference. The Radio Division maintained a central monitoring station at Grand Island, Nebraska; nine secondary monitoring stations; and six mobile units' mounted on trucks, for field investigations. These mobile units were capable of acting as mobile direction finding (DF) units.

In 1932 Congress proposed that the president be authorized to transfer the duties, powers, and functions of the Radio Division of the Department of Commerce to the Federal Radio Commission, where it became the Division of Field Operations. When the Federal Communications Commission assumed the property of the Federal Radio Commission in 1934, the Division of Field Operations became the Field Division. Under the FCC, radio monitoring activities were expanded. The number of mobile monitoring stations designed primarily for measuring the field strength of stations but adaptable for DF and other field work, was raised to nine. Monitoring transmissions, identifying stations, and supplying intercepts to interested government agencies continued. Various changes, extensions, and improvements in FCC radio monitoring activities were made in ensuing years, and the Department of Justice, the Coast Guard, the State Department, and the Army and Navy came to place varying degrees of reliance upon the FCC in matters involving illicit use of radio.[56]

In September 1940, J. Edgar Hoover queried the possibility of the FCC monitoring all long-distance telephone calls between New York and Germany, France, and Italy. He also suggested that since Japanese, French, Italian, German, and Soviet officials were sending both foreign language and encrypted communications via cable, it might be well for the FCC to obtain copies of all encrypted and unencrypted communications which might have a bearing on our national defense problems. These suggestions created legal and administrative problems for the FCC, and at Chairman James L. Fly's request, a meeting was held in January 1941 between the FBI and the FCC's Chief Engineer and General Counsel to iron out the problems.[57]

The FBI was interested in all communications between the Western Hemisphere and Germany, and in December 1940 requested that the FCC cover the Chapultepec, Mexico, commercial transmitter for ten days as "information [had] been received from a confidential source that the station [was) communicating with Germany." Fly apparently wanted to drop the assignment after ten days, but FBI director Hoover informed him that "the continued submission of this material is important to the national defense investigations being pursued by this Bureau." The FCC continued the assignment, and on 8 February 1941, Hoover requested another sixty-day extension of the mission. On 28 February, Hoover informed Fly that collection of Chapultepec could be limited to its communications with Germany, New York, and Rocky Point, Long Island. In April the Coast Guard requested that the FCC collect the communications between Chapultepec and Nauen, Germany. This was later expanded to include all Chapultepec-Germany communications, an assignment modification in which the FBI concurred.[58]

In January 1941, the FCC, which had been tasked by the Defense Communications Board with monitoring foreign press and propaganda broadcasts, sought an additional fund allotment of $304,120 for the remainder of fiscal year 1941. These funds were to be used by the FCC's National Defense Organization (NDO) to establish the Foreign Broadcast Monitoring Service (FBMS), including the purchase of additional technical equipment and the hiring of translators and political analysts.[59]

The additional appropriation was approved and the FBMS was established. The FCC appropriation request for fiscal year 1942 exceeded the total fiscal year 1941 request by $300,000. Of this increase, $150,000 was requested for modernization of monitoring equipment, and $150,000 was requested for additional personnel. In modern terms such an increase is infinitesimal, but in 1941, $300,000 represented a sixteen percent increase in the FCC appropriation.[60]

The British Effort: GC&CS and the RSS (1919-1941)

The British cryptanalytic effort in World War II was centralized in the Government Code and Cipher School (GC&CS) which had been established by the British government in 1919 to study foreign cryptosystems and to advise on the security of British cryptosystems. It was originally made up of twenty-five officers recruited from the remnants of the World War I Admiralty and War Office cryptanalytic sections and was placed administratively under the Admiralty. In 1922 GC&CS, together with the Special Intelligence Service (SIS), was transferred to the Foreign Office, and in 1923 the head of the SIS was redesignated "Chief of the Secret Service and Director of GC&CS."[61]

When GC&CS was established, the War Office and the Admiralty reserved the right to remove their personnel at need to man their own SIGINT centers. By 1935, however, it was realized that the production of SIGINT was a continuum of processes which could not be separated. This, together with the earlier decisions to centralize peacetime

cryptanalysis, was a strong argument in favor of maintaining the same organizational structure in wartime. The Cryptography and Interception Committee of GC&CS, which included representatives of the three services, had a standing subcommittee, the Y Subcommittee, which coordinated the services' radio intercept activities.[62]

During World War II, the British intercept effort against Axis clandestine communications was conducted by the Radio Security Service (RSS). This organization was tasked with identifying and performing the initial intercept of Axis illicit stations communicating with Germany. The original intention was that the intercept organizations of the various services would assume the burden of intercept after the nets had been identified by the RSS. In practice, because of the intercept load already being carried by the services, the RSS became the organization responsible for the intercept of Abwehr communications, by far the most extensive of the illicit nets.[63]

The origins of the RSS extend back to 1928, when the Committee of Imperial Defence charged the War Office with the responsibility for creating an organization for detecting illicit radio transmissions within the British Isles. The original concept was that such an organization would be directed and financed by the War Office, with personnel and equipment provided by the Government Post Office (GPO). This concept received official approval in 1933.[64]

The normal responsibilities of the GPO with regard to radio communications were very similar to those of the FCC in the United States, i.e., enforcement of the laws concerning radio operation; overseeing amateur radio operation; policing frequency usage; and investigating the causes of radio interference. In a paper written in 1938 for MI-5, Lieutenant Colonel Adrian F.H.S. Simpson pointed out that the GPO's effort against illicit transmissions was merely an offshoot of its primary operations, and any economies achieved through the use of the GPO would be false ones from a military point of view. MI-5's objectives were to prevent unauthorized transmissions; to collect transmitted messages for examination and decryption; to locate the transmitting stations; to prevent, in some cases, the receipt of unauthorized signals within the country; to conduct research into new or unusual methods of transmission; and, above all, to watch over a much larger range of frequencies than that proposed by the GPO. The GPO's objective, on the other hand, was to wait until the law was broken and then to determine the cause. This difference in philosophies was to plague the British effort for some time.[65]

The new organization for the Interception of Illicit Wireless Communications (IWI) was tasked with intercepting illicit signals originating in, or directed toward, the British Isles. It was soon recognized, however, that there were also illicit signals which were originating abroad and were directed toward Germany. The War Office decided in July 1939 to establish intercept sites abroad to collect these signals. Three sites each were to be established in Egypt and Tanganyika; two each in Palestine, Malaya, and Gibraltar; and one each in Malta, The Cameroons, Aden, and Hong Kong. All sites were all under service auspices.[66]

MI-5, as the organization responsible for the defense of the realm, was not involved in the work of IWI (redesignated MI-1(g) in 1939) until after an illicit transmitter had been located. At this point, MI-5 became responsible for coordinating seizure and arrest. It was decided, therefore, that in cases of suspected espionage, MI-5 would control procedure and all liaison with the police. In such cases, the police would be given no details concerning MI-1(g) organization and would be impressed with the need for delicacy and discretion in their inquiries.[67]

In an attempt to tighten collaboration between MI-5 and MI-1(g), the War Office intercept organization was revised in September 1939. MI-1(b), the department responsible for military intercept, was reconstituted as MI-8, under the jurisdiction of the War Office and the Director of Military Intelligence (DMI), and MI-1(g) became MI-8(c). That part of MI-8(c) concerned with the intercept and identification of illicit transmissions was renamed the Radio Security Service (RSS).[68]

At first, the only illicit signals originating from the British Isles were the transmissions made by an MI-5 double agent codenamed SNOW. By January 1940, three radio groups had been identified and were ready to be turned over to the armed forces intercept services, better known as the "Y" services. One of these, a shipboard station anchored near Bergen, Norway, was identified through its communications with SNOW, and was taken over by the Admiralty "Y" service. Another group was of interest to the French. The third, the worldwide Abwehr net, appeared to be too large a task for any of the already overloaded "Y" services, and in the end, the RSS assumed responsibility for its intercept. Traffic was forwarded to GC&CS at Bletchley Park, Bedfordshire, where a special section was established for handling the cryptanalysis of illicit systems. This section was known as Intelligence Services, Oliver Strachey (ISOS), after its chief. In a later division of responsibility, ISOS was made responsible for the analysis of hand systems. Intelligence Services, [Dillwyn] Knox (ISK), was made responsible for the analysis of the higher level machine systems. The small amount of Abwehr traffic encrypted on the TUNNY system, referred to as ISTUN, was decrypted by the TUNNY Section.[69]

In May 1941 the headquarters organization of the RSS was transferred to MI-6, and the overseas intercept units followed in August. Operations were directed by a steering committee made up of representatives of MI-5, MI-6, GC&CS, and the three armed services. This organization remained essentially unchanged for the remainder of the war. The mission of the RSS was recognized as consisting of the detection, collection, location, control, and suppression of all Axis clandestine radio operations, worldwide.[70]

Bletchley Park's Victorian mansion, which housed Great Britain's cryptologic efforts

The Reorganization of the U.S. SIGINT Effort (1939-1942)

Executive memoranda of 1939 had ordered the centralization of SIGINT in the Army, Navy, and FBI. The cabinet secretaries were instructed to see to it that any such activities in their departments were handed over to these three organizations, the directors of which were to function as a committee for coordination of intelligence activities.[71]

Later in 1939 Roosevelt ordered that all crypt-analytic efforts likewise be centralized: those in ONC, the United States Army Signal Corps, and the FBI. He also directed that a communications intelligence committee–the CI Committee–be constituted with one representative from each of these organizations, to serve in an advisory capacity to the Intelligence Committee designated in the 26 June memorandum.[72]

Although the committees were formed, little of the centralization appears to have been accomplished, and it took an outside event to stimulate a change. On 2 April 1942, a confer-ence was held at the State Department, chaired by Assistant Secretary of State Adolf A. Berle and attended by representatives of the Army, Navy, State Department, FBI, and FCC. The direct occa-sion for the meeting was a Brazilian police roundup of enemy agents in Rio de Janeiro on 18 March. The arrests were premature but were apparently made at the suggestion of the U.S. embassy, which had promised to provide the police with decrypted messages as evidence. The next day, the U.S. naval attaché in Rio de Janeiro requested copies of all intercepted and decrypted messages relating to the CELALD group of agents, so-called because of their radio callsigns.

The Navy considered it dangerous to release such information. However, since the embassy was deeply involved, the Navy agreed to supply the evidence with certain caveats. Since the attaché already had decrypts, no more would be sent until a decision was made on the releasability of the information, and the attaché was to withhold those in his possession until then. A check was to be made to determine whether the police had seized any messages in their raids, as that would simplify cover. In any case, the only messages to be supplied would be those in a cryptosystem which had been superseded on 18 September 1941. As will be seen later, these precautions went for naught.[73]

Admiral T. S. Wilkinson, the CNO, asked Berle to call the conference in order to establish a general policy for such disclosures. In his letter to Berle, Wilkinson expressed a fear that any of the agencies handling such traffic could, in the absence of a general policy, take unilateral action detrimental to the interests of the United States or to the other agencies involved, including British and Canadian authorities. Wilkinson believed that the Department of State should be the determining authority as to the action to be taken with regard to information derived from intercept, since inaction could result in continued receipt of information and would avoid the risk of enemy knowledge that their cryptosystem had been broken.[74]

The participanta at the meeting decided that the danger of closing down a vulnerable source of intelligence precluded revelation of radio intercept except in the most serious cases and tasked Major General George V. Strong, the Assistant Chief of Staff, G-2 (A.C. of S., G-2) with drafting a statement to serve as the basis of an Executive Order. He forwarded the following text to Berle on 3 April.

> *No action toward the closure of international clandestine radio stations or apprehension of individuals engaged in clandestine radio communications in which there is any military or naval interest, or actions requiring disclosure of intercepted communications, shall be initiated without the joint approval of the Chief of Staff of the Army and the Chief of Naval Operations, or their designated representatives.*[75]

At the 2 April meeting, FCC Chairman Fly called attention to the duplication of effort and incomplete coverage resulting from improper coordination of the efforts of several cryptographic bureaus. At that time, in addition to the Army, Navy (including Coast Guard), and FBI organizations, there were cryptanalytic units, existing or planned, in the FCC, the office of Censorship, the Weather Bureau, and the Office of the Coordinator of Information (COI) (later the Office of Strategic Services–OSS). The Navy representative at the meeting, Commander John R. Redman, recommended that the Coast Guard assume responsibility for all cryptanalysis not performed by the Army and Navy, but no unanimity of opinion could be reached and the matter was referred to the Intelligence Committee.[76]

At an Interdepartmental Intelligence Conference on 8 April, it was agreed that there would be a conference on the subject of intercept responsibility. Representatives at the conference were to be Mr. D. M. Ladd (FBI), Colonel John T. Bissell (MID), Commander John R. Redman (ONC), and Lieutenant Commander Alwin D. Kramer (ONI). Late in April, this subcommittee, augmented by Colonel Carter W. Clarke (MID), Commander Joseph N. Wenger (ONC), and Mr. E. P. Coffey (FBI), took up the question of coordination, and cooperation in the cryptanalytic work of the three services and the question of the processing of coded intercepts.[77]

The division of effort at this time was as follows:

- Navy (including Coast Guard)–enemy naval, enemy diplomatic, enemy clandestine, and potential enemy naval and diplomatic;

- Army–enemy field military, enemy diplomatic, enemy commercial, and potential enemy military and diplomatic; and

- FBI–enemy diplomatic, enemy commercial, enemy clandestine, espionage, shore-to-ship, and U. S. criminal.

In addition, the FCC had attempted some elementary cryptanalyis to guide collection.[78]

Taking into acccount the recommendation of the subcommittee, Admiral Wilkinson, as chairman of the Joint Intelligence Committee, recommended to the Joint Chiefs of Staff (JCS) on 18 June 1942 that presidential approval be obtained to eliminate all cryptanalytic efforts in agencies other than Army, Navy, and FBI.[79]

Another coference subcommittee was appointed, made up of Colonel Carter W. Clarke, Colonel Frank W. Bullock, and Mr. William F. Friedman for the Army; Commander John R. Redman, Commander Joseph N. Wenger, Lieutenant Commander Alwin D. Kramer, and Lieutenant Commander L.T. Jones (USCG) for the Navy; and Messrs. E. P. Coffey and D. M. Ladd for the FBI. This subcommittee recommended the following allocation of work:[80]

Diplomatic	Navy
Enemy Naval Operations	Navy
Enemy Military Operations	Army
Western Hemisphere Clandestine	FBI/Navy
Other Clandestine	Navy
Trade Codes	as assigned by the committee
Army Weather	Army
Navy Weather	Navy
Domestic Criminal	FBI
Voice Broadcast	FBI
Cover Text Communication	FBI
Miscellaneous	as assigned by the committee

The recommendation was forwarded to the president on 8 July by the JCS, and by the president to the director of the budget on 8 July with instructions to implement. A memoraadum to Mr. B. L. Gladieux of the Bureau of the Budget on 18 July stated that neither the OSS nor the State Department was conducting cryptanalytic activities, but that there were small units in the office of Censorship aad the War Communications Board

(part of the FCC), both of which were reluctant to turn staff and equipment over to the Army aad Navy. After the application of some pressure by the Bureau of the Budget, the Office of Censorship informed the Director of Budget on 12 August that Censorship's cryptanalytic unit had been abolished and fourteen persons were being transferred to the Navy Department to continue their work. On 1 September, the Director of Budget informed the president that with the FCC agreeing to discontinue plans for employing cryptanalysts, all responsibility for cryptanalysis had been vested in the Army, the Navy, and the FBI.[81]

Initial Operations

From July 1940 to May 1941, the FCC had provided the State Department with copy from clandestine stations in Mexico, Venezuela, Colombia, and Iceland. On 15 July Chairman Fly had forwarded to the DNC a number of encrypted messages which had been copied and sent in to the FCC by amateur radio operators. In return, the Navy was forwarding traffic the FCC had intercepted by naval radio stations which appeared to fall under the cognizance of the FCC. Among these was an encrypted message intercepted at Jupiter, Florida, on 8 August as it was traasmitted from an unidentified station to "AOR." The latter was to be one of the major "controlled" Axis agent transmitters.[82]

As far as the Coast Guard was concerned, the FCC intercept was useful at first only for collation purposes and for filling in some of the gaps in Coast Guard collection. As FCC operator efficiency improved, however, it became a valuable source of original material. An agreement was reached between the two organizations in April 1942, whereby the FCC began to provide traffic from all clandestine circuits, particularly those operating out of Argentina.[83]

As a result of the declaration of a state of emergency, the Coast Guard was resubordinated to the United States Navy on 1 November 1941 and after some discussion, the Cryptanalytic Unit followed in March 1942. It did not, however, become a part of OP-20-6 until 1 March 1943, when it was moved from Coast Guard Headquarters to the Naval Communications Annex and designated OP-20-GU. In this guise, and with a staff of twelve, it continued the work on German clandestine systems which it had started in 1940. By July 1943 the unit had been enlarged to twenty-three persons and, as a part of the Navy cryptologic organization, was tasked with the reception, identification, and collation of clandestine transmissions; the analysis and solution of clandestine cryptographic systems; the translation and editing of decrypted clandestine material and the preparation of this translated material for dissemination; and liaison with the British intercept and cryptanalytic organizations in connection with clandestine traffic.[84]

The Coast Guard was receiving all of the intercepted clandestine traffic passing to and from South America, but had little or no DF capability, relying on the FCC and the Navy for this service as well as for assistance in intercept. After decryption and translation by the Coast Guard, copies of the translations were disseminated to the Navy, the Army, the State Department, the FBI, the FCC, and the COI. The FCC, acting on information received from the Coast Guard, obtained DF bearings on the clandestine transmitters. In accordance with the April 1942 agreement, the FCC furnished the Coast Guard with intercepted traffic from all clandestine and suspected clandestine circuits. U.S. Navy DF stations in the Caribbean also collected German clandestine traffic, obtained DF bearings on terminals in the Western Hemisphere, and conducted continual search for other clandestine stations. This information was then passed on to the Coast Guard. The FBI, which performed little or no intercept on its own, assembled data from both the Coast Guard and the FCC, added information from its own files, and prepared reports for the State Department.[85]

The Coast Guard was operating three intercept stations on the East Coast when the war began, and these, together with the Navy sites at Toro Point, C.Z.; Winter Harbor, Maine; and Jupiter, Florida, were its main sources of clandestine traffic. Unfortunately, because the Navy operators were unfamiliar with the problems of copying clandestine transmissions, the material furnished by the Navy stations was of little or no value to the Cryptanalytic Unit. Commander Jones was convinced that if the Navy operators were indoctrinated in proper collection procedures at the Coast Guard station on Long Island, and if OP-20-G were to decide to make a real contribution, the situation would change. In the meantime, FCC traffic was "only fair," traffic from the British was weeks late in arriving, and the Army exchanged traffic only out of courtesy and not regularly. As a result, the Cryptanalytic Unit was left with the task of performing cryptanalysis on traffic from nets which were very incompletely covered.[86]

Security Problems

In mid-July 1940, ONC informed the FCC that "somewhere in the United States a station on approximately 14,370 kc. is transmitting information to agents in Europe regarding the departure of vessels from the port of New York." Two stations were involved in the communications: one using the fixed callsign "AOR," and the other using daily-changing calls. The latter was referred to throughout the ensuing events as "UK" (unknown) or, from its call-up procedure, "VVV TEST."[87]

George Sterling, as chief of the FCC's Radio Intelligence Division (RID), immediately instituted a conference call with the FCC's primary monitoring stations at Baltimore, Maryland; Hingham, Massachusetts; Grand Island, Nebraska; Portland, Oregon; and San Pedro, California, requesting that they be alert for such transmissions. The first FCC intercept of the link was accomplished at the Portland monitoring station on 2 August 1940.

The science of HF direction finding was still in its infancy, and the FCC was further handicapped in locating these stations by a lack of Adcock-type direction finders. Navy DF "fixes" were confused by the Navy's inability to distinguish between the two ends of the link. Thus, on 8 August 1940, the Navy reported that the clandestine station was located in west central New England or New York State. Subsequent inconclusive DF reports giving bearings of 42 degrees from Pensacola, Florida, and 49 degrees from Amagansett, New York, and a report on 6 September placing AOR near St. John, New Brunswick, were of little help.[88]

On 17 September, Admiral Noyes informed the FCC that both AOR and N7Z had been identified and no further intercept was required. (N7Z was a British cruiser in U.S. waters, completely unrelated to AOR.) Since the Army, which had been given copies of the messages, was also uninterested in the traffic, this left only the FBI as a user of the FCC intercept on this link, and the FBI was providing no feedback.[89]

It was becoming increasingly apparent to the FCC that VVV TEST was located in the United States, probably in New York State, but the FBI denied this possibility. Sterling, therefore, again approached the Navy in November and provided them with intercept of more than 100 messages. Navy interest was reawakened, and OP-20-G began a cryptanalytic attack on the traffic and began providing additional DF. These bearings, combined with FCC bearings, placed the station near New Haven, Connecticut. An FCC team was placed in the area with mobile DF units, and on 7 December 1940 the station's location was pinpointed in Centerport, Long Island.[90]

Earlier in the year, the FBI had requested an unlisted, confidential, amateur radio station callsign assignment for a station to be located in Centerport. Consequently, on 9 December Sterling notified Hoover of the clandestine station's location. The FBI denied that there was anything special about the Centerport station but admitted later in the day that the clandestine station was part of a highly successful counterespionage operation.

At this point, the FCC officially closed the case on VVV TEST-AOR but continued to copy all transmissions and forward the intercept to the FBI for record purposes. In January 1941 the FBI tasked the FCC with collecting another station, GLENN, located just outside Mexico City, which was using the Centerport station as a relay to communicate with AOR.

The FBI could not decrypt the traffic from the Mexican station and passed it on to the Coast Guard for analysis. Since the traffic passed to the Coast Guard was from Mexico to Germany, with a relay through the United States, the Coast Guard instituted its own collection of the group pursuant to its duties with regard to the monitoring of unneutral communications in the Western Hemisphere. The Coast Guard also asked the Army for copies of back traffic from the VVV TEST-AOR circuit as an aid to analysis. When the Army replied that all of the traffic had been returned to the FCC, the Coast Guard queried that agency. The FCC replied that it would search its records and immediately notified the FBI, which gave assurances that the situation would be explained to the Coast Guard.[91]

In fact, the Coast Guard was told merely that the station in Centerport was being covered by the FBI, with no mention that the station was FBI-controlled. This did not become known to the Coast Guard until July 1941, when thirty-three Axis agents were arrested by the FBI and the story of the FBI-controlled spy station was released to the press. According to Captain J. F. Farley, the Chief Communications Officer of the Coast Guard,

> *Up to that time the information transmitted by this station had been found sufficiently accurate that we had no suspicion that it originated from other than genuine espionage agents. The accuracy of ship information transmitted by this station was as high or possibly higher than would be expected from diligent and faithful espionage agents.*[92]

In fact, the Coast Guard was of the opinion that the information supplied to the Germans by the FBI via the VVV TEST-AOR circuit was so accurate that its value to Germany could not be overestimated. Captain Farley pointed out specifically that a message concerning the ship *Ville de Liege* named only the one vessel and stated that she was sailing without convoy. After the *Ville de Liege* was sunk, the sailing date named in the message was one of the most important features in the trial of the German agent Kurt Ludwig. The FBI agents involved asserted that they had decrypted and read every message sent by TEST; thus they were responsible for having transmitted that one. Farley considered the fact that the VVV TEST-AOR circuit was operated for nearly eighteen months, until its termination by the FBI, to be proof of its value to the Germans.**93**

The Coast Guard Cryptanalytic Section was able to solve most of the messages sent from Mexico to. AOR via VVV TEST. These messages provided considerable information concerning the activities of Axis agents in Latin America and links to other communications groups which were being studied at the time. As a result, the Coast Guard continued monitoring the group, although VVV TEST was, of course, no longer operative.**94**

From a security point of view, just as important as the information provided to the Germans by the FBI was that information concerning the readability of the cryptosystems used on this circuit had been released to the press. This was not to be the last time that the service SIGINT organizations would protest against FBI procedures in handling communications intelligence. As time went on, the Coast Guard became convinced that some of the agencies receiving verbatim texts of clandestine messages, particularly the FBI and the State Department, were too free in their use of this information. In February 1942, as a result, the Coast Guard ceased distribution of verbatim texts to all agencies other than ONI and the British Security Coordinator (BSC–the British Intelligence liaison office in New York City), sending free translations

to the others. This measure was, unfortunately, taken too late. The Navy attempt to reduce the impact of the release of clandestine SIGINT in connection with the round-up of Axis spies in Brazil was futile because the Department of State had already provided the Brazilian government with voluminous files of verbatim texts, including copies of all the messages from Brazilian circuits which were in the possession of the FBI.

The messages provided to the Brazilians by the FBI through State Department included hundreds of decrypts provided to that agency by the Coast Guard from the Rio de Janeiro-Hamburg circuit. The FBI's only source of intercepted traffic at that time was the monitoring network of the FCC. As it happened, the South American end of the circuit could not be heard in the United States, where all of the FCC stations were located. About 500 messages originating in Rio de Janeiro had been copied by U.S. Army monitors in Brazil and had then been forwarded to the Coast Guard for decryption and translation, making the Coast Guard the only source for this material. To a certain extent, this was true of all the information supplied by the FBI on South American circuits, since material decrypted by the FBI was usually worked on the basis of cryptologic information supplied by the Coast Guard.

Providing this information to the Brazilian authorities resulted in Brazilian officials showing decrypted verbatim texts to German agents during interrogation. In one instance, a prisoner was asked to assist in the translation of obscurely worded messages. The fact that the systems used on all clandestine circuits were completely changed almost immediately indicates that the Germans had thus been informed that their cryptosecurity had been breached.**95**

The FBI Connection

Initially, Coast Guard relations with the FBI were cordial. Under the original 1942 agreement, OP-20-GU continued working on the systems then being read by the Coast Guard; the FBI continued working on the systems they were reading, and the two consulted before beginning work on new systems. In addition. to ensure some measure of control over FBI cryptanalysis, it was agreed that the Navy and the FBI were to confer on coordination of work on Western Hemisphere clandestine material. The Navy had made no commitments on anything other than Western Hemisphere clandestine.

When in February 1942 the FBI, MID, and ONI signed a secret agreement concerning the establishment of a DF network to locate clandestine radio stations in Latin America, MID assumed responsibility for location of clandestine stations in Latin American countries and dissemination of the clandestine information obtained to the FBI and ONI. The Navy, therefore, no longer considered itself bound to supply FBI with any clandestine information at all. Not only did the Navy consider that its relationship with FBI had netted practically nothing, but as time went on it became increasingly apparent that while the FBI was demanding everything that OP-20-GU had, it was withholding potentially valuable information from that organization. Relations continued to deteriorate, beginning with the New York spy trials and the Brazilian spy roundup.[96]

In January 1942 representatives of BSC met with U.S. naval officers to discuss clandestine intercept. The British attitude was that since these stations could never be completely suppressed, it was better to allow them to operate so that they could be monitored. At this meeting it was decided to hold weekly conferences at the Coast Guard Communications Office, the participants being representatives of OP-20-G (after 2 February 1943), the RSS, and the Coast Guard Cryptanalytic Unit, with occasional attendance by representatives from Canada and from the Radio Intelligence Service (RIS) of the U.S. Army.[97]

Shortly after Pearl Harbor. the RSS asked to exchange information with the Coast Guard Cryptanalytic Unit. As a result, weekly exchanges were made with the RSS representative in the United States. Somewhat later a similar arrangement was made with GC&CS.[98]

The FBI objected to the RSS-Coast Guard exchanges. They cited their agreement with BSC, to which the RSS representative was attached for administrative purposes, and demanded that the RSS deal with American agencies only via the FBI. The British were forced to agree and the exchanges were terminated. The GC&CS representative, however, was not included in the agreement, and Coast Guard exchanges with him continued.[99]

Prior to the 1942 conferences assigning SIGINT responsibilities to specific agencies, the Army and Navy had hoped that the FBI could be persuaded to retire from the cryptanalytic business and agree to turn that duty over to the services. They hoped in vain, however. Because of Hoover's reputation and power, the best result that could be obtained was to confine the FBI to domestic criminal and Western Hemisphere clandestine communications.[100]

Several months after the termination of the RSS-Coast Guard liaison, the British expressed dissatisfaction with the accuracy of the information they were receiving from the FBI, implying that they would be forced to resume liaison with the Coast Guard. The FBI then proposed that the Coast Guard, RSS, FCC, and FBI hold weekly discussions of clandestine monitoring problems. The other agencies agreed, with the proviso that they were free to contact one another outside of the weekly meetings. These meetings, to discuss Western Hemisphere monitoring problems, were conducted for several months; the RSS and Coast Guard representatives met later to discuss the clandestine problem outside of the Western Hemisphere. There were relatively few Western Hemisphere circuits, and their communications were relatively unchanging, so there was little to discuss at the FBI meetings. After a few months the meetings appeared to be a waste of time, and the Coast Guard and RSS ceased attending. From then on, the FCC was notified of any communications changes, allowing them to keep their logs current for the Western Hemisphere. The RSS and Coast Guard weekly meetings continued, and FCC logs were sent to all parties.[101]

In 1943 the Coast Guard solved the Enigma system used by a clandestine station in Argentina, and began working other Enigma links whose setups had been provided by the Signal Security Agency (SSA). In view of the poor security procedures of the FBI, which received copies of the Coast Guard solutions, the nature of this system was brought to the attention of OP-20-G. As a result of the MID-FBI-ONI Agreement, Colonel Carter Clarke of G-2 had said that the FBI should no longer be supplied intelligence resulting from clandestine communications except through G-2, and the Army and the Navy agreed that the messages were not to be provided to the FBI. Instead, ONI would provide the FBI with summarized information which would conceal the source. Immediately after this decision was reached, an urgent message was received from the British expressing their fears for the security of Enigma solutions if they were provided to the FBI. They were reassured that the FBI would not receive any intelligence that would compromise the work being done on Enigma.[102]

The Enigma served as the standard cipher machine for Germany's military, its agents, and its secret police.

By the end of 1943, the presence of information in the ONI summary which had not been received by the FBI as individual decrypts indicated to Hoover that there was a quantity of Western Hemisphere SIGINT to which his organization was not privy. He complained to Rear Admiral R. E. Schuirman, the DNI, that the Navy, by withholding verbatim translations, was interfering with the FBI in the accomplishment of its mission of controlling the operations of enemy agents in the Western Hemisphere. He claimed that the FBI had been providing the Navy with intercepted messages, but the product from these intercepts had not been furnished to the FBI.

Hoover's attitude was that the Navy's refusal to provide the FBI with this material would force him to close down the operations of the Argentine and Mexican agent nets. He realized that this was not as desirable as allowing them to operate in a "supervised" fashion, but he could see no alternative. If this action became necessary through the failure of the Navy department to make the messages available to the FBI, he would, "of course," have to "explain to the proper authority why such action must be taken."[103]

The DNI replied to Hoover that the information which the Navy was producing from communication intelligence activities was being used to the greatest extent possible, bearing in mind the necessity of avoiding revelation of Allied cryptanalytic success. The use made of such information had to be secondary to the safeguarding of such success. As a consequence, the verbatim text of messages solved by the Navy were not being given to anyone who did not have an urgent need for them and who was not also subject to control by the Navy as far as enforcement of necessary regulations for safeguarding the information was concerned. The DNI further stated that if Hoover decided that it was necessary to seize foreign agents who were transmitting information from Argentina to Germany, he requested that Hoover advise him before taking such action. He pointed out that if the FBI did this, it would be necessary to inform Argentinian authorities and such information would certainly find its way to Germany. He concluded with the statement that if the FBI, in negotiating with the Argentine authorities, revealed or even suggested that messages currently being transmitted from clandestine stations were being solved, then the FBI would have furnished Germany with information of such value as to seriously conflict with the national interest. The Navy did not back down from this position, and, fortunately for everyone, Hoover did not carry out his threat.[104]

The Army Connection

Early in 1942, the SIS started a traffic analytic study of German clandestine communications, using traffic received from the FCC; the Army's intercept stations at Ft. Hancock, New Jersey, and Rio de Janeiro; the Brazilian government's intercept service; the 120th SRI Company in the Canal Zone; and the 123rd SRI Company in Cocoa, Florida.

The Army's effort consisted primarily of circuit identification and the solution of preamble keys. No effort was made, apparently, to perform cryptanalysis on the message texts.

The reasons for this work were presumably to keep the Army abreast of developments in clandestine radio communications in order to correlate them with other traffic analytic and intercept control problems and to furnish a nucleus in the event the Army had to take over the problem.[105]

In late 1942, GC&CS agreed to provide the SIS with the "Schedule" and the "RSS New Services and Amendments," the two documents published by the RSS to keep their intercept operators informed of changes in Abwehr communications. The Navy called G-2's attention to the fact that clandestine communications were a Navy responsibility under the terms of the Army-Navy-FBI agreement. G-2 agreed but stated that the Army did not consider that Abwehr communications between Berlin and Rome, for example, were clandestine. The Army

view did not take into account the fact that the Berlin-Rome link was part of a net that included Turkey, Spain, and Portugal, but since G-2 stated that the Army was engaged in only research, the Navy did not press the matter. On or about 15 July 1943, the Army operation was abandoned and records were no longer maintained.[106]

As a result of the decisions made after June 1939, all analysis of the clandestine problem was the responsibility of the Coast Guard and the FBI until the end of the war. Analysis is, however, only one phase of the SIGINT process. Intercept and location of the Axis stations were performed by not only the Coast Guard and the FBI, but also the Navy, the Army, and the FCC; and coordination of the various efforts was to remain a problem throughout the war. One of the attempts at this was the creation of the Joint Radio Intelligence Centers, of which only the first, in San Francisco, had any real connection with the clandestine problem.

The Radio Intelligence Center

On 9 and 10 January 1942, a series of meetings was held at Headquarters, Western Defense Command and Fourth Army (WDC), at the Presidio of San Francisco. These meetings were attended by representatives of WDC, 12th Naval District, the FCC, and the FBI. Their purpose was to plan a joint facility for the coordination of radio intelligence information.

This Radio Intelligence Center (RIC), as the facility was to be called, was created to collect, evaluate, and disseminate intelligence related to the identification and location of radio stations; for surveillance of radio transmissions; and for interservice exchange of radio security information. It was to be totally operated by the FCC with the services having tasking authority and providing liaison personnel. All information obtained was to be provided to the services and to other FCC customers.

The initial planning called for direct teletype communications between the RIC and the NDO, the FCC's primary stations in Portland and Santa Ana, the Office of Naval Communications, and the Signal Intelligence Service of WDC. In addition, there was to be teletype exchange (TWX) service for other stations and direct telephone service to the Joint Command Post, the Office of Naval Communications, and the Signal Intelligence Service. An emergency radio station was also to be installed.[107]

The major incentive for creating such a center appears to have been provided by Lieutenant General John L. DeWitt, commanding WDC. On 14 January, DeWitt called Colonel Freeman Raymond in Washington, D.C., to request Raymond's assistance in expediting the funding for the center. DeWitt told Raymond that he intended that the Army should fund the operation for at least the first eighteen months, because going to the Navy for money would slow things down. He commented that the Navy was, along with the Army, concerned with the DF fixes that were being obtained on shortwave stations that the Japanese were using all along the coast to communicate with their submarines and surface ships.[108]

Although DeWitt was demanding immediate action, there ensued a delay while everyone in the chain of command avoided making a decision. Although the. Chief' Signal Officer and G-2 appeared to be in favor of the operation, the War Department wanted more Navy cooperation and expressed the belief that DeWitt's problems could be solved by providing him with a direct telephone link to the FCC in Washington. Finally, on 5 February 1942, an affirmative decision was made by G-2 and the War Department was asked to approve the funds. The requests for direct teletype circuits and an emergency radio station, however, were to be reviewed after it had been determined whether or not such installations were justified. In the meantime, TWX circuits would be used, although WDC felt they would be unsatisfactory. After the funding approval by the War Department, imple-mentation of the decision was rapid. And the RIC, located in the Federal Building in San Francisco, was placed in operation on 1 March 1942.[109]

Chapter 4

Counterclandestine DF Operations in Latin America

Introduction

In addition to the cryptanalytic and reporting effort directed against Axis agent communications, continuing attempts were made to determine the location of enemy agent transmitters through high frequency direction finding (DF). Interest was particularly high in finding these stations in Latin America, and two major attempts were made, first by the U.S. Navy and then by the FCC and the U.S. Army, to establish DF operations in that area. As it happens, the documentation of the history of these two attempts is far more complete than is the documentation of the history of the cryptanalytic effort. In both cases, the operation was based on the training of indigenous personnel to man the sites with U.S. personnel serving as advisors. The success of these two operations was mixed.

The U.S. Navy in Colombia and Ecuador (1940-1941)

The Navy's first experience with Axis clandestine communications started in 1940. In May and June of that year, Ecuadoran authorities intercepted a number of transmissions from unidentified stations, apparently within Ecuador, passing four-letter and two-figure encrypted traffic and some apparent German plain text. Fearing Axis clandestine operations, Ecuador asked the United States for technical aid in locating illegal radio transmitters in their country. This request was for equipment only, but Boaz Long, the U.S. ambassador to Ecuador, recommended (probably with Ecuadoran government approval) that in addition to the Adcock DF (direction finding) equipment requested, two radio receivers and nine radio personnel be sent.

At about the same time, Colombia made a similar request as a result of a conference early in 1940 between the American minister at Bogotá, the U.S. Army mission in Colombia, and the Colombian government. In this case the request was for two U.S. radio operators, two Adcock DF systems, a portable DF, and a high-frequency receiver, with the idea that Colombian personnel would man one of the Adcocks and the portable DF with the U.S. personnel manning the remaining Adcock and HF receiver and training the Colombian operators. This request was referred to the Navy Department, as no other branch of the U.S. government had any high frequency direction finding equipment or technical knowledge of the subject.

The Ecuadoran intercept had been the first tangible evidence of the existence of a Nazi radio net in Latin America. Commander Safford of OP-20-G, to whom the request had been referred, concluded that on the basis of the frequency information provided by Ecuador, it was possible that there was a continent-wide radio net in direct communication with Germany. Safford did not believe that the Adcock direction finders were suitable to the terrain found in Colombia and Ecuador unless highly trained operators were also provided. The Navy offered to help find the transmitters, using direction finders located in U.S. possessions, if information were provided concerning the schedules and frequencies of the clandestine stations. Such information was not provided, but the American minister repeated his recommendation and the Colombian government made a direct request for the assistance. Upon the recommendation of the State Department and the approval of the president, the Navy Department agreed to furnish the equipment requested in order to show token cooperation with the Latin American republics.

Since he had been ordered to comply, Safford suggested following the Communications War Plan, already carefully worked out and approved. He recommended that a small-scale operation be initiated, using such personnel and equipment as were available, and that this operation be placed under the direct control of the U.S. naval attachés in the two countries and the Commandant, 15th Naval District, Canal Zone. The Navy would make up existing deficiencies and issue the necessary directives. Safford recommended that one Model DT high-frequency DF and one RAS high-frequency receiver be transferred to 15th Naval District, to be manned by U.S. naval personnel in Bogotá; that four loop¬antenna portable direction finders be obtained commercially and shipped to the same command for loan to the Colombian and Ecuadoran governments; and that the Navigational Direction Finder Station at Bethany Beach, Delaware, be closed and decommissioned, thereby making personnel available so that four radiomen could be sent to 15th Naval District for detail to Bogotá and the high-frequency DF at Balboa, C.Z. Safford reckoned that the Adcocks at Bogotá and Balboa could get cross bearings on targets for general location and the mobile DFs, manned by local military personnel, could then determine the exact location of the transmitters.[110]

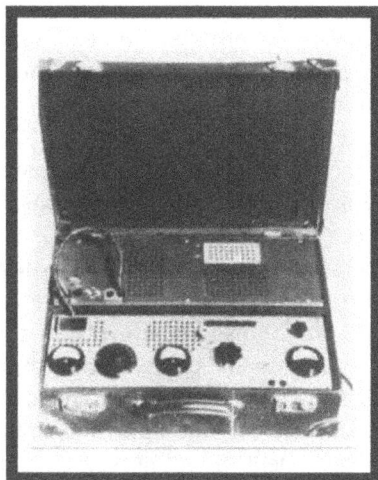

Portable radio used by Nazi agents in South America

Safford's concept of operations was for the most part rejected by the U.S. ambassador in Bogotá, who thought that the use of mobile DFs manned by U.S. Navy operators in Colombia might prove an embarrassment to the Colombian government. The ambassador suggested that a fixed site be established within the U.S. chancellory, using one receiver, and that the other receiver and the DF be loaned to Colombia to be mounted in government trucks and operated by Colombian operators under U.S. Navy guidance.[111]

Safford argued that he had assumed that the original request for assistance had come from the Colombian authorities, but that it now appeared that they had not given approval. He insisted that the plan be implemented as proposed on 25 June, stating that neither Colombia, the U.S. ambassador, nor the U.S. Army mission had sufficient experience with high-frequency DF to make intelligent changes to that plan. Furthermore, no equipment should be landed in Colombia until a qualified officer from 15th Naval District had gone to Bogotá and made all the necessary arrangements with both Colombia and the U.S. naval attaché. These arrangements would include such things as the licensing of both truck and transmitter, detailing of Colombian support and operating personnel, legalization of the status of the U.S. operators, and arrangements for funding. After the Colombian government was assured that it would have full authority and full responsibility for the equipment, that the United States would not infringe on Colombian sovereignty, and that the Navy operators would be evacuated as soon as they had taught Colombian operators to use the equipment, the plan was approved.[112]

The CNO ordered the equipment assembled on 16 July for shipment to 15th Naval District. All major items except the RAS receiver were to be provided by the U.S. Coast Guard, which was to be appropriately reimbursed. On the same day, the CNO ordered the Commandant, 15th Naval District, to send a qualified officer to Bogotá to make arrangements and to activate the Balboa DF station. Once arrangements with Colombia were made, similar arrangements were to be made with Ecuador.[113]

In return, the commandant reported that the Balboa DF could not be activated as there was no site suitable for its location. As a result of his suggestions, navigational service was suspended at the Toro Point and Cape Mala intermediate frequency direction finders; the operating personnel were sent to the Coco Solo Naval Air Station to man the Type DT-1 DF there for "strategic" purposes, and the Type DT direction finder at Balboa was resited at the David Naval Air Station. Later, the Coco Solo DT-1 was relocated at Toro Point and a Type DY direction finder was sent to 15th Naval District to be used for strategic high frequency DF. This last equipment was sited at Farfan Radio Station and assigned a staff of fifteen.[114]

Pursuant to the CNO's orders, the 15th Naval District Communications Officer, Lieutenant Commander F. K. McElroy, reported to the U.S. ambassador in Bogotá on 7 August 1940, and met with Sr. Castro y Martinez, the Colombian minister of war, the next day. Castro desired that the U.S. naval operators be assigned to the U.S. Naval Mission at Cartagena and then detailed to Bogotá as instructors and that the equipment also be transferred to Cartagena and carried on the naval mission books. Somewhat earlier, on 4 August, the ambassador had informed the State Department that it was essential for the radiomen to be technically assigned to the naval mission, not only because this was in accordance with his verbal agreement with President Santos but also because it would have a tendency to prevent undesirable publicity. As additional cover, the Navy radiomen would wear civilian clothes and live on the economy near the embassy. Communications would be by daily cable schedules between Cartagena and Balboa and between Bogotá and Quarry Heights, C.Z., with direct communications between Bogotá and Balboa to be arranged later. The truck would be licensed as a Colombian government vehicle and painted to resemble other Colombian Army

Air Corps trucks, with gasoline, oil, and repairs taken care of by the Colombian Army Air Corps. Two Colombian Army Air Corps officers, Colonel Ernesto Buenaventura and Captain Alvaro Roldan, had been assigned as supervisors and had completed most of the preparations.

After his arrival, McElroy informed the Commandant, 15th Naval District, that the Colombian Army Air Corps had four French D.M.T. Type RC-7 portable DF equipments which were inoperative. McElroy had arranged for the Balboa radio station to repair one set and recommended that all four sets be put in working order, as he thought it would improve cooperation if Colombian equipment could be used as part of the operation.[115]

The radio trucks were shipped to Panama on 20 August aboard S.S. *Santa Clara*, out of New York. One truck, accompanied by RM1/C Jones Atkins, Jr., and RM2/C Thomas C. Warren, arrived in Bogotá in early October. On 8 October Atkins and Warren informed OP-20-GX of initial hitches resulting from dilatoriness on the part of Colombian authorities and also complained that they had not been paid. In the meantime, Lieutenant (j.g.) Joseph E. Johnson had reported to OP-20-GX for temporary duty while awaiting orders to proceed to 15th Naval District to supervise the operation.[116]

The operations in Ecuador and Colombia never really got off the ground. The Navy was determined that its personnel would be assigned as teachers only, in spite of McElroy's insistence that the personnel provided by the local authorities were not competent to operate or maintain the equipment. McElroy was firmly of the opinion that the only way the operation could be productive was to have all the work done by U.S. operators. Ambassador Long concurred in this opinion.[117]

McElroy's reports were not well received in Washington and on 2 January 1941, the CNO stated that the Navy had agreed to supply equipment to both Ecuador and Colombia together with two naval personnel each to train the native operators, and that the Navy intended to follow the official agreements to the letter and had not authorized any encroachments on the rights and responsibilities of the two countries. When the Navy subsequently received a report that the Ecuadoran minister of war wanted the DF equipment in the country to be operated entirely by U.S. Navy operators, Captain Schuirmann requested that State Department ask the Ecuadoran government to take over the operation of the DF and to provide Ecuadoran operators for training since the use of U.S. operators alone was considered undesirable by the Navy.

As to intercept of the clandestine net, there was some question in Washington about the validity of the intercept coming from the DF operation in Ecuador, inasmuch as the traffic logs received appeared to consist of rebroadcasts of code messages originating at the German naval radio stations at Kiel and Nauen. In some cases the naval transmissions were repeated verbatim; in others various prefixes, suffixes, and internal numeric groups were added. In addition, it was not possible to match the intercept logs with any entries on the DF logs. These Latin American stations could not be heard at Cheltenham, Maryland, or Jupiter, Florida; and when it was discovered that 15th Naval District had not attempted to monitor this traffic, the DNI ordered such tasking to be implemented straightaway.[118]

On 7 January Lieutenant Commander Greenacre, the naval attaché in Quito, made a trip to Guayaquil, where the DF operation had been set up, to investigate the situation there. The ostensible reason for this trip was to investigate an attempt on the life of Radioman Smith, who had been shot on 2 January while operating a mobile DF in the jungle about ten miles from Guayaquil.

As a result of his investigation, Greenacre reported that the U.S. operators were in a dangerously exposed position and recommended that the operation be closed down until more adequate

quarters for both men and equipment could be obtained.

A far more serious matter than the attempted shooting was the problem of the validity of the material being collected. Although circumstantial evidence indicated that the messages intercepted in Guayaquil were invalid, intercepts submitted by RMI/C Harrison in July 1940 in Quito indicated they were genuine. (Harrison had been detailed to Quito in July from the U.S. Special Service squadron and had been commended for his work in Ecuador by the squadron commander.) In Ecuador, the connection between DF and intercept was, to say the least, tenuous. The DF operation, while it performed some tasks as required by 15th Naval District, was largely self-directed, with reports apparently being passed to Washington via the naval attaché and the 15th Naval District. Morale of the operators was low, and their dedication to their work left a great deal to be desired. Administrative procedures were poor, logs were not properly kept, and working hours were vaguely defined.

The situation with regard to intercept was, if anything, worse. Intercept duties were performed by an ensign of the Ecuadoran Navy, Jorge Washington Castillo, who operated receivers both at home and at the office of the Captain of the Port. The traffic logs were passed from Castillo to a Frenchman resident in Guayaquil who turned them over to the British consul. The British consul, in turn, furnished copies to the American consul, who forwarded them to the American legation in Quito, which turned them over to the naval attaché, while forwarding a copy to State Department. The attaché forwarded his copy to 15th Naval District and made and forwarded a copy to ONC in Washington.

Monitoring at Cheltenham, Maryland, and Jupiter, Florida, over a period of eight months and the observations of the DF trucks had failed to substantiate the Guayaquil messages. In an attempt to resolve the situation, Greenacre sat "side-saddle" on the intercept position with Castillo long enough to convince himself that the ensign's logs and traffic bore little resemblance to what was actually being heard. When Castillo claimed he was copying local stations in South America, he was actually copying high-powered naval stations in Germany. In addition, his log for 10 January showed him recording the three-letter U.S. Navy calls, NPM and NPG, as three two-letter calls, NP, MN, and PG, of unknown stations. Harrison, the previous year, had apparently also copied the German naval stations, altered the copy, and claimed it to be from local stations.

In spite of all this, Greenacre felt that the reports of clandestine radio stations came so consistently and from such varied sources, that this, together with the shooting of Smith, indicated that there was a clandestine operation in Ecuador, possibly either in very limited operation or on standby status.

Greenacre added his recommendation to previous ones from McElroy and various intercept operators, stating that he believed that turning the DF equipment over to Ecuadoran operators with U.S. operators as instructors would mean the end of all secrecy and chances of success in the project. He said that every American and Ecuadoran official who was aware of the project and with whom he had discussed the point had concurred in this opinion. He believed that if Ecuadoran operators were allowed to handle the gear except under the direct and immediate supervision of a qualified American operator, it would soon be beyond repair. He did think that continuing on the basis of direct and open instruction of Ecuadoran operators on the chance of stumbling upon a clandestine station might be worthwhile for (1) the good will value involved and (2) the possible value of having U.S. personnel on the spot in the event that a change in the international or internal situation might bring the clandestine stations into greater activity.[119]

As a result of Greenacre's investigation, Safford recommended on 27 January that the Ecuadoran unit be disbanded and evacuated from Ecuador. Safford felt that most of the Navy's problems

in Ecuador were due to the interference of the American minister, Boaz Long, who had submitted Castillo's intercept logs as evidence supporting the need for a DF unit and had pressured McElroy to accept an arrangement that was decidedly disadvantageous to the Navy. Greenacre's investigation had shown that the intercept logs submitted by Long were false, and thus there was no evidence of clandestine radio in Ecuador. On 2 February 1941, U.S. DF operations in Ecuador were suspended and the volume of intercept, apparently from Castillo, increased markedly. Although the attaché considered this to be suspicious, Colonel Rodriguez, the Ecuadoran Zone Commander, placed full credence in the intercepted material.[120]

On 5 February the Commandant, 15th Naval District, informed CNO that Radioman Smith had forwarded a "coded intercept" intercepted by Castillo. The translated text of the message which had been transmitted by station "HC" read:

CODE DESTROYED STOP RADIO WILL BE DISMANTLED AFTER THIS TRANSMISSION TOMORROW READY FOR TRANSPORTATION SANTA ELEANA PENINSULA OBSERVATIONS NEXT WEEK. DAYBREAK YESTERDAY NAUEN RECEIVED BULLET RIGHT LUNG DIED THIS AFTERNOON STOP TRIED TO INTIMIDATE NAVY OPR. HC COOPERATING WITH US AGAINST THIS SHOOTING BELIEVE MAN NOT LIABLE TO BRIBERY ONLY REPRISAL.[121]

In the absence of other information regarding this message, two questions come to mind. Since it apparently refers to the Smith shooting (Smith had managed to wound one of his attackers), why did Castillo not mention it to Greenacre during his visit to Guayaquil? The memorandum from 15th Naval District states that Balboa's translation, shown above, was slightly different from Guayaquil's. If, as the memorandum states, this was a "coded intercept," how was Guayaquil, or for that matter Balboa, able to read it? One possible answer is that the Americans never saw the coded version, but only Castillo's plaintext version, which may or may not have had any validity. Certainly, the next day Safford informed OP-20-A that OP-20-G was thoroughly convinced that not only were the Guayaquil intercepts fraudulent but Harrison's intercepts were also suspicious. On 4 April Safford requested that radiomen Smith and Chance be transferred back to 15th Naval District and two high-frequency DF operators be sent TAD to Quito.[122]

Smith and Chance were transferred, but it was some time before they were replaced. On 11 August 1941, the chief of the U.S. Naval Mission to Ecuador recommended to CNO that the equipment be turned over to the Ecuadoran Navy and located in Quito; that the two radiomen due to be transferred to Ecuador be instructors only, assigned to the Naval mission and able to speak Spanish; that it be publicly stated that the equipment had been loaned to Ecuador for the instruction of naval personnel; that the U.S. Navy write off the equipment; and that Ecuador be made to understand that any information received regarding clandestine radio was to be made available to the U.S. Navy Department. In October the DNC commented that he was willing to turn the equipment over to Ecuador as soon as that country qualified for lend-lease and requested the transfer. If this qualification did not materialize, he was then willing to write off the equipment when appropriate. The DNC concurred in the other recommendations made by the Chief of the Mission, noting that he assumed that since U.S. operators would know what was being intercepted, the information would be available to the U.S. Navy. [123]

In contrast to the situation in Ecuador, the Colombian unit was functioning in a satisfactory manner by late January 1941, although no clandestine radio stations had been verified. McElroy considered that the lack of success in Colombia was a result of the determination of the Navy Department that the U.S. operators be used only as instructors.

Another explanation was provided by the FBI on 1 February when Director Hoover informed Assistant Secretary of State Berle that he had information that a German radio station had been operating in Bogotá during the first three weeks in January. He told Berle that the reason for the lack of success of the American radio operators in Bogotá who were trying to locate this station was the fact that the Colombian Army officer in charge of the operation was in the pay of the Nazis and was reporting all of their actions to the German minister to Colombia. (Note that this apparently referred to Captain Roldan.)

Hoover's letter was passed on to OP-20-G, where Safford stated that it was so vague that comment was impossible and requested the FBI to provide more complete information and a copy of the original report. After considerable delay, the DNI answered Hoover's letter on 11 June. He noted that the detail of U.S. Navy operators and equipment to Colombia was not an attempt to encroach on an FBI preserve, but had been done at the request of the Colombian government, with the personal approval of President Roosevelt. He pointed out to Hoover that in the formal analysis, the responsibility for suppressing clandestine broadcasts rested with the local authorities and not with either the U.S. Navy or the FBI. As for Captain Roldan, he had been placed in charge of the operation by the Colombian authorities. The charge made by Hoover was a serious one and, if substantiated, should have been made known to the Colombian authorities via the State Department.

As of 11 March, Captain Roldan had detailed only one operator for training. McElroy informed U.S. ambassador Spruille Braden that even if Roldan detailed the three additional radio operators he had promised, it would take several months to train them. In addition, he questioned whether the Colombians would ever learn to operate or maintain the equipment properly. He recommended the assignment of a sufficient number of U.S. and Colombian operators to permit continuous watch standing on the DF and the receiver; continuous manning of the portable DF when a specific station was being investigated; and assignment of an experienced chief radioman to handle training and overall supervision. This would mean an establishment of twelve men, six of whom would be Colombian. He also recommended an increase in the number of personnel assigned to the Balboa DF to provide for three continuous intercept watches there.

McElroy considered the use of Colombian operators, all of whom were civilian, to be dangerous from the point of view of security. This, combined with the necessity for the U.S. to exercise indirect control over airport and aircraft communications, made it advisable to exert pressure on Avianca, the Colombian national airline, to have its eligible personnel enlisted in the U.S. Naval Reserve, and to have a communications officer attached to the embassy for liaison with the Colombian Communications Section and with Avianca and Panagra (Pan-American Grace Airways).[124]

Orders were sent to the Bureau of Navigation on 4 April to effect the paper transfer of radiomen Atkins and Warren from the 15th Naval District to temporary duty at the Office of the Naval Attaché in Bogotá. Atkins, however, had become involved in a drunken brawl in Bogatá on 27 May and was sent back to Balboa on the 29th by request of the ambassador and the Colombian government. Warren had been sent back to Balboa on or about 3 April, apparently because of personal differences with Captain Roldan.[125]

The Colombian government requested that both operators be replaced and that a "trained crew" be transferred to Bogatá. Safford recommended that Colombia be informed that the Navy Department would prefer not to replace its DF operators at Bogatá. This reaction was occasioned by several factors, primarily the fact that the duty was undesirable from the point of view of the operators because of living expenses, low pay, and lack of companionship. Added to this was the anomalous status of the operators and the overall lack of cooperation by Colombian authorities in establishing a DF operation controlled by Colombians.[126]

The Colombian foreign minister had expressed to the United States ambassador his regrets that nothing had been accomplished by the operators and equipment and his conviction that part of the information possessed by the totalitarian legations could not have been obtained through ordinary channels. In his comments on this conversation, Safford pointed out that inasmuch as only one Colombian had ever been assigned to the DF (and he did not learn to operate it) and the U.S. operators had been withdrawn at the request of the Colombian government, there was no one in Colombia who could operate the equipment to produce the desired results. As to the foreign minister's conviction, the possession of extraordinary information by the totalitarian legations merely proved that they had radio receivers through which they received information from transmitters in Europe, and the DF equipment could not track down receivers. The Navy had no evidence of illicit transmitters in Colombia.

Once again, Safford would, if ordered, detail replacement personnel, but he was unalterably opposed to increasing the size of the detachment or including an officer in the unit. If sent, the operators were to be attached to the Office of the Naval Attaché. In any case, the Navy was agreeable to leaving the equipment in Bogatá on a loan basis.[127]

Atkins and Warren were replaced by Chief Radiomen Thomas R. Cullen and Everette G. Fowlkes, who were directly subordinated to Ensign Joseph Fox, of the Office of the Naval Attaché. As of 27 October 1941, the DF operation was housed in a satisfactory location near the Avianca Air Field and the RAS receiver was installed in the house occupied by Cullen and Fowlkes. Roldan had again promised to provide five operators for training, but had actually assigned only one man, the operator trained by Atkins and Warren. Cullen and Fowlkes informed the Communications Security Section of CNO on 27 October that the naval attaché had been ordered by the ambassador to actively engage in tracking down clandestine stations and that that was what they had been doing. The two chiefs noted that if results from that part of their assignment were desired, then additional qualified men should be assigned, since the operators Captain Roldan would provide would not be qualified for such a task. The CNO noted, once again, on 23 December, that the naval radiomen were sent to Colombia as a political gesture for duty as instructors, and that the DF in Colombia was intended to operate independently under the control of the local government and not as a part of any DF net under U.S. control.[128]

After his inspection trip to Colombia in October 1940, McElroy had gone on to Ecuador. At that time he had predicted to Lieutenant Commander Greenleaf that the Ecuadoran government wanted to pay for nothing in connection with the DF operation and it would be necessary to provide U.S. funds for expenses connected with the truck. McElroy had also advised that cash should be advanced to Atkins and Warren in Colombia to minimize overt Navy involvement, but Bureau of Ships stated that such expenses were chargeable to radio station maintenance funds in 15th Naval District. Such funds could not be advanced on the basis of an estimate, but issued only after a determination had been made of the amount required for the remainder of the fiscal year. Such a request had to originate with the Commandant, 15th Naval District, and be forwarded to Bureau of Navigation for CNO approval.[129]

McElroy thought that handling the project through the Supply Department of the Bureau of Navigation had already made it "known to the whole world." Furthermore, the poor mail service made the forwarding of the required vouchers quite difficult. Apparently the problem was never resolved.[130]

In August 1941 DNC had requested that orders be issued transferring Chief Radiomen Harry I. Maltz and Raymond H. Bradford to Ecuador. During the interval between Smith's departure and the arrival of the new team, there had been an extensive shakeup in the Ecuadoran military

high command, with the consequence that none of the new incumbents knew about the DF operation. Since the new command was pro-American, Greenacre did not consider this to be any great problem. He was worried, however, about the wording of the team's transfer orders, which said that Maltz and Bradford were to "report to the Chief of the Naval Mission for duty under the naval attaché." Greenacre noted that this was akin to "reporting to the USS *Misouri* for duty on the USS *Idaho*" and requested clarification.[131]

For some not readily understandable reason, there was strong opposition in Washington to any change in the wording of the orders or clarification thereof. A memorandum from Bradford to the Communications Security Branch of CNO on 31 October recommended that the unit be assigned to the mission and that the chief of the mission be authorized to issue travel orders. On the copy of this memorandum received by OP-20-G there is an underlined "NO!" written in next to this recommendation. Bradford's request had been occasioned by the fact that the team, which had been in Ecuador for nearly a month, had not yet been able to commence operations, as its status had not been cleared by CNO.[132]

As of 2 December, the Navy was still maintaining its position regarding the duties of the team, the respective responsibilities of the U.S. and Ecuadoran governments, and its desire to pull the operators from Ecuador for reassignment. As of the same date, Bradford had reported to CNO that the team had done no DF work since arrival. The equipment was in satisfactory condition but could not be tested because all the batteries were dead. Bradford and Maltz had reported to the assistant naval attaché, Lieutenant E. J. Beall, and had stood watch in Beall's house for approximately eleven days, from 21 November to 2 December, to try to intercept clandestine transmissions, with no result. Ensign Castillo had intercepted clandestine traffic on 15 November, for the first time in many weeks.[133]

Safford did not get around to answering Greenacre's earnest request for clarification of orders until 17 December 1941. His letter simply reiterated the rules under which the operation was to be conducted and stated that the Navy was trying to get the DF operators transferred to the naval mission with the intent of moving them back to the United States as soon as possible. He closed by commenting that since the United States was now at war, the matter of the Ecuadoran DF team was far from being a first priority consideration. In January 1942 the decision was made to return Bradford to the United States and to leave the equipment in Ecuador to be turned over to the local authorities as lend-lease as soon as Ecuador qualified and so requested.[134]

Other Latin American Nations before the War

Aside from the DF operations in Colombia and Ecuador, and occasional DF of clandestine radio at Balboa and Guantanamo Bay, Cuba, there was very little Navy involvement in the Nazi clandestine radio problem preceding World War II.

While the Navy was implementing its plans for operations in Colombia and Ecuador, the U.S. legation in San Jose, Costa Rica, reported that the Costa Rican Ministry of Security had requested equipment and an expert to find secret radio broadcasting stations believed to be operating in that country. This request was passed on to OP-20-G, which stated that the DF equipment that was being relocated in the Canal Zone would be able to cover Costa Rica and that the Navy's long-distance radio direction finder stations would eventually be able to establish the general locality of all clandestine radio stations operating in Central and South America. The Navy, of course, would inform Costa Rica of stations determined to be within its borders, and these could then be tracked down with locally manned loop-type DF. The Navy said they would try to provide such equipment to Costa Rica within about six months.[135]

In Cuba, Major Juan V. Govea, Director of Public Radio, Cuban Department of Communications, had stated informally on 2 December 1940 that Cuba urgently needed equipment to detect the presence of foreign aircraft, to watch radio and telegraph communications, and to set up radio beacons for air control. His primary aim seemed to have been to control propaganda coming from outside the country. Much later, in September 1941, the State Department suggested that the Navy establish some intercept sites in Cuba, apparently to aid that government as the Navy was doing in Colombia and Ecuador. The Navy informed the State Department that the idea of setting up intercept stations in Cuba was overambitious, since Navy Department requirements were being met by present and prospective U.S. stations in the area. However, the Cuban authorities could, on their own, set up an FCC-type operation. This would benefit the United States by helping suppress Nazi clandestine radio stations in Cuba, but the project would have little additional value to the United States, since the U.S. Navy radio station at Guantanamo Bay adequately served U.S. requirements.[136]

In the case of other Latin American countries, the only SIGINT-related activities prior to the entry of the United States into the war were conducted either through the U.S. establishment in the Canal Zone or through reports to U.S. naval attachés. This situation would change radically with Pearl Harbor and the declaration of war against Germany and Japan.[137]

Establishment of the AIS Clandestine Radio Locator Net

The American Intelligence Service (AIS) was an agency of the Intelligence Group, Military Intelligence Service, charged with the collection, completion, and primary evaluation of military, political, economic, and psychological information pertaining to the Western Hemisphere south of the United States. One of its specific tasks was to maintain a branch for Special Intelligence, including dossiers on known subversive suspects in Latin

America and studies and analyses of enemy espionage systems in Latin America. It was under this charge that U.S. Army intercept and DF operations directed against Axis clandestine radio operations fell.[138]

After the fall of France and the Netherlands, American authorities began to worry that Dutch or French possessions in the Western Hemisphere, or some isolated area such as the upper Amazon, might be used as military bases from which to launch a surprise attack on the Panama Canal or the United States. There was also a fear that with the initial Axis successes in North Africa, a military landing of some size might be attempted on the northeast coast of Brazil. Such actions might be augmented by an Axis "fifth column" in Latin America.[139]

Creation of the Concept, December 1941-January 1943

With U.S. entry into the war, increased fears of Axis clandestine operations in the Americas resulted in a 30 December meeting at the State Department to discuss suppressing clandestine radio. At that meeting, State Department representatives pointed out that the problem of clandestine radio was serious, involving a chain of communications all over the Western Hemisphere routed to the Axis countries through Martinique and Dakar. Any attempt to identify, locate, and close down illicit transmitters would thus have to be a hemisphere-wide one. This would require the cooperation of local authorities, since although DF operations could be conducted from the United States, the bearings obtained would not be sufficiently accurate for the purpose. Location of the transmitters would require the establishment of local DF units.

Admiral S. C. Hooper, Director of the Radio Liaison Division within the Office of the CNO, proposed that a resolution be introduced at the Rio Conference, to be held 15-28 January 1942. This resolution proposed that the countries of Central and South America agree to suppress clandestine radios and to cooperate with other countries to that end; to create a committee of representatives from the countries involved for the exchange of technical information; and to create a technical committee for planning purposes. Implementing such an operation would require purchasing portable direction finding equipment to be used in each country and ten fixed-site, long-range direction finders to be placed as needed. The resolution also called for each country to send one or more representatives to the United States for training by the FCC in direction finding and intercept. The meeting also accepted the suggestion by Thomas Burke, of State Department's Division of International Communications, that a committee be created composed of representatives of the FCC and the War and Navy Departments under the chairmanship of Admiral Hooper, to determine all the necessary technical details concerning the equipment to be purchased. This committee met in Admiral Hooper's office on 1 January 1942.[140]

Resources had already been mobilized within the United States for the purpose of suppressing clandestine radio operations in the Western Hemisphere. Both the Coast Guard Intelligence Unit and the FBI were, as we have seen, tasked with the cryptanalytic side of the problem. And the FCC was actively intercepting clandestine circuits. By the end of 1941, the National Defense Operations Section (NDO) of the FCC was intercepting Axis clandestine circuits operating between Lisbon and Portuguese Guinea and between Lisbon and Mozambique, as well as transmitters operating with Rio de Janeiro and Valparaiso. The NDO had located seventy-five individual clandestine stations, four of them in Brazil. The Navy had noted clandestine cipher transmissions from South America to Germany, beginning around the middle of 1941. By mid-February 1942, five distinct groups had been noted, two of them operating out of Brazil and one out of Chile. As a result of conversations with representatives of the BSC, the British Army, and the British government, the Navy had concluded that the British were intercepting the same traffic.[141]

After the 1 January meeting, Admiral Hooper informed the State Department of the DF equipment necessary to carry out the counterclandestine operation. At a minimum, any organization that would be established would require fifty automobile-mounted mobile DF units, four airborne units, and ten fixed-site DFs to be used as base stations. The rationale for the estimate was that the base stations would initially detect and locate target transmitters within a circle of 50-100 miles. A more accurate determination could then be made by an airborne unit, with ground-mobile units providing the final "pin-down." Hooper suggested suitcase-type DF units with a 1,600-18,000 kHz capability and a range of twenty to fifty miles for the automobile units and aircraft receivers with carrier level meters and a 200-30,000 kHz capability for the aircraft. Purchase prices for these systems would be approximately $400 each for the automobile units and $1,000 each for the airborne units. The fixed-site DFs would be Adcock-type direction finders loaned by the Navy and built by the Collins Radio Corporation. They would have an effective frequency range of 2,500 to 18,000 kHz. In addition to the DF equipment, each airplane would be equipped with ordinary transmitting and receiving equipment. Each base station would require a two-kilowatt high frequency transmitter costing $7,000, a receiver costing $1,000, and auxiliary equipment for frequency determination and communications with the associated intercept site.[142]

The ten Collins DFs would cost $45,000 each and were of the newest and best type of Adcock DF equipment. On 2 January, Lieutenant Commander George W. Welker of OP-20-GX pointed out to Lieutenant Commander F. C. S. Jordan that none was available at the time since first deliveries were not expected until February and that Navy requirements would probably absorb the first year's production. The Army was also in no position to provide the equipment required. Welker considered DT and DY direction finders to be quite adequate for the purpose envisioned, and in the end these were the types deployed.[143]

The FCC's initial concept of personnel and equipment requirements for the operation were, as it turned out, ridiculously small. On 25 February S. W. Norman, the Acting Chief of the NDO while George Sterling was on TDY to Hawaii, informed the State Department that the requirement would be for two monitoring officers skilled in DF, two portable loop DFs with azimuthal scales and tripods, two Hallicrafter B-29 receivers, two aperiodic receivers, and two "body receivers." Norman did say that more men would possibly be needed later, up to a total of eight or ten, but that the additional personnel would probably be provided by the Coast Guard.[144]

The desired resolution was introduced at the Rio Conference and was adopted as Resolution XL (Elimination of Clandestine Stations). Brazil and Chile stated that they considered the situation to be serious and urgent, and requested U.S. aid. The State Department replied that two men with equipment would be sent by the FCC as soon as the two countries agreed to the U.S. proposal. Although there were objections within the Signal Corps to FCC involvement, these were apparently not voiced at subsequent planning sessions.[145]

As a result of the adoption of Resolution XL, a committee was organized under the chairmanship of Thomas Burke. This committee was charged with designing a program to cope with clandestine radio stations in Latin America. The committee included representatives of the Signal Corps, the Army Air Force, the Navy, the Marine Corps, the FCC, the State Department, and the Director of Inter-American Affairs. The committee met on 11 March to define the problems to be solved.[146]

The Technical Committee, which was appointed at this meeting, met on 16 March and prepared recommendations on the technical aspects of the problem and on the desirable locations for the ten base stations.

The recommendations were presente to a meeting held in Burke's office at the State Department on 19 March. Norman, as chairman of the Technical Committee, presented its report recommending placing base stations in the vicinities of Bahia de Salinas, Rio Grande do Sul, and Rio de Janeiro, Brazil; Valdevia, Arica, and Santiago, Chile; Callao, Peru; Santa Elena (Salinas), Ecuador; and the Falkland Islands. The Navy would provide Adcock DFs for these sites, as well as the fifty suitcase equipments that were required. Commander Jordan suggested that since transmitters for interstation communication would be difficult to obtain, the organization could buy Hallicrafter 100-watt transmitters for $200 apiece. Lieutenant Commander Joseph W. Fowler stated that ONI was in favor of sending U.S. personnel to man the stations but pointed out that actually getting rid of clandestine stations was a problem for the local authorities. Commander Welker suggested that the organization should take advantage of the equipment left in Colombia and Ecuador by the Navy in 1941. As a final note, the representatives of the Coordinator of Inter-American Affairs (CIAA) stated that if a complete plan were developed and presented, CIAA would be willing to finance the entire operation.[147]

On 22 May Burke called a meeting at his office for the purpose of discussing the FCC training course for the South American technicians which was to start 8 June at the FCC Monitoring Station at Laurel, Maryland. Ten Latin American republics were sending a total of eighteen men for training (Guatemala, Mexico, and Ecuador did not participate). The State Department had informed the governments of the American republics that the U.S. would pay all expenses incurred by nominees to the course, including travel and maintenance, and that the United States would provide all the republics with the equipment necessary to accomplish the objective.[148]

Vice Admiral A. W. Johnson of the Inter-American Defense Board had called an informal meeting of Army and Navy representatives on 10 April. They had discussed the fact that no agency seemed to be in charge of the Latin American operation. The conferees agreed that one agency should take over responsibility and one man should direct the operation.[149]

The FCC representatives at the 22 May meeting were caught by surprise when Admiral Johnson suggested that the FCC's NDO administer the Latin American project, as their understanding was that the FCC was responsible only for training; but they abstained from comment. Burke agreed with Johnson that the program should be administered by someone who was technically qualified and agreed to call a meeting of the FCC, War Department, and Navy Department to obtain their recommendations.

The Navy had already started a program of modifying their DY direction finders to improve their design, but at this meeting Admirals Hooper and Johnson suggested that the FCC should make the modifications to the DYs destined for South America. Norman stated that since these were Navy improvements to a Navy design, the Navy was better equipped to do the job.

Upon being informed of the above, Chief Engineer Jett approved of FCC running the program, suggesting that George Sterling and Philip F. Siting attend the forthcoming meeting and that Sterling administer the program.[150]

Another meeting was held on 7 July, with only War and State Departments participating, in which it was decided that the War Department would undertake the direction of the project, under the general supervision of the G-2, Major General George V. Strong. At about the same time, the DNC agreed that the project should be under State/Army control.[151]

By 18 July the training course was well underway, although Sterling considered that a large part of it was being wasted since the portable DF units being supplied by the Navy were nothing like the sets the FCC was using for training and the Navy sets would have to be modified.[152]

At this point, Sterling estimated that the FCC would have to send ten engineers to Latin America to assist in setting up the project. Sterling also informed Jett that additional personnel would be required in the United States to handle the projected receipts of traffic from the Latin American net. It is evident from Sterling's memorandum to Jett on 18 July that the FCC had agreed to accept the additional responsibilities suggested by Admirals Hooper and Johnson. That this was most acceptable to everyone is evidenced by a letter from Assistant Secretary of State Breckenridge Long to Chairman Fly giving effusive thanks for the work being done by the FCC. As a result of a meeting held on 14 July, it had been decided that the project would be administered by an interdepartmental board composed of representatives from State, FCC, CIAA, and the Navy, under the general direction of the War Department's MID. It had also been decided that the headquarters for the operation would be located in Mexico City. Fly rejected the concept of a Mexico City headquarters, suggesting instead that Mexico City be the reporting center and Washington, D.C., the administrative center for the organization.[153]

Colonel S. P. Collins, the MIS liaison officer for the Latin American program, called a meeting on 20 August at which equipment and personnel were the primary subjects of discussion. Collins reported that three Adcock DFs were available for shipment, and one each had already been installed in Colombia and Ecuador (apparently the DFs left behind by the Navy). Five others were in the process of being overhauled and would be shipped about 1 September. At that time, ten 100-watt transmitters, thirty Hammarlund receivers, several frequency meters, and other equipment would be shipped. Each shipment would be addressed to the U.S. mission in the country of destination and the FCC engineers would be scheduled to arrive soon after their equipment.

Although the plan called for the shipment of fifty portable direction finders, it was up to the countries concerned to provide the vehicles for installation. In fact, the two trucks which had been left behind in Colombia and Ecuador should be returned to Panama and not turned over to the host governments. It was feared that if the trucks were given to Colombia and Ecuador, other countries would find out and resent not receiving similar treatment.

It was noted that on 15 August, Sr. Banegas of the Honduran Department of Investigation had requested DF assistance. The FCC stated that two Finch loop DFs were available, but that DF in Honduras was highly impractical since the country had no roads.

In marginal notes on Norman's memorandum concerning this meeting, Jett indicated approval of the statements concerning equipment and the request to retain Robert Linx in Brazil (see below). He also agreed that it would be necessary to send one man to each country after the equipment had been delivered and suggested letting the Hondurans buy their own loop DFs; otherwise, every country would expect the FCC to provide them gratis.[154]

On 13 October Colonel Collins and Commander Jordan called on Sterling to discuss the project. As a result of this meeting, the concept of the plan, at least as far as FCC thinking was concerned, was rather thoroughly revised.

In his memorandum to Jett on the meeting, Sterling made a number of complaints about the way things were going. Primarily, he felt that Collins and the State Department had not been keeping the FCC aware of their thinking and planning. Collins had explained to him that the FCC was to have no part in processing intercepted material and was not to provide any coordination in the operation of the Latin American monitoring stations. The War Department was establishing a DF station in Miami for this purpose, and Collins had already set up his headquarters in a hotel there. The MID was training Army personnel in traffic identification and would send them to the Latin American stations. The FCC was expected to send engineers to set up the stations and render engineering assistance. This would, apparently, end the FCC obligation. Sterling thought that the FCC engineers were going to have considerable problems as far as equipment was concerned, and that if the Army was going to run everything else, it should also be responsible for the engineering. He particularly objected to the Army making the FCC responsible for the installation and operation of the DY direction finders, which the FCC considered deficient and unreliable.

Sterling told Jett that a few days previously H.E. Otterman had brought him a memorandum that Collins had sent Francis de Wolfe describing the proposed distribution of equipment. Otterman had been quite surprised to find that neither Sterling nor Norman had been advised of this proposal, which was at variance with the original plan. Otterman informed de Wolfe of the situation and the latter got in touch with Collins, who said he would be receptive to any suggestions the FCC might make. Collins had then accepted an FCC plan that had "due regard for the base lines required in order to secure proper cuts." (The final locations of these base stations were Bello Horizonte, Brazil; Talcahuano, Chile; Bogotá, Colombia; Ciudad Trujillo, Dominican Republic; Quito, Ecuador; Yucatan Peninsula, Mexico; Callao, Peru; Montevideo, Uruguay; Puerto Cabello, Venezuela; and Miami, Florida.)

In conclusion, Sterling recommended that the FCC withdraw its offer to lend engineering services, since it appeared that none of the essential elements of the project would be under FCC control. "If it works out well, Army and Navy will get all the credit; if it comes out bad, we will take the rap." The next day an article appeared in the *Baltimore Sun* concerning Argentina's inability to get equipment to detect illegal radio stations. Sterling's comment to Jett was

> *It is rather distasteful for me to be associated with a group who has such little comprehension of the*

> *problem and knowledge of equipment with which to accomplish it, and [with] the dillydallying in trying to get organized for the purpose of doing something about it.*[155]

He went on to say that if the FCC had had full responsibility, the equipment would be in Argentina and operational.

After selecting the first four men to go to South America, Sterling had discussed the assignment with a number of others through early September. At that time he had predicted that the assignment would involve a sixty- to ninety-day tour of duty abroad. On that basis, a number of monitoring officers had expressed interest in the assignment. When in mid-September he informed them that it would be at least a six-month detail, several changed their minds.

Three men had been dispatched in March. In answer to a request from Assistant Secretary of State Berle, Robert D. Linx and John F. de Bardeleben had been ordered to proceed to Miami on 16 March for onward transport to Rio de Janeiro and Santiago, respectively. (It had been decided that Brazil's request for aid in suppressing clandestine stations within that country was not in pursuance of the overall goals of the project.) On 21 March Sumner Welles, the acting secretary of state, had transmitted to the FCC a request from the Cuban Government for the loan of technical equipment for the detection and suppression of clandestine radio. Fly had informed Welles that only a limited supply of equipment was available, but that the FCC would try to accommodate the request. The Navy had also met with the Cubans on 20 March in regard to the same request and had agreed to lend equipment until the Latin American project became a reality. Welles repeated the request to the FCC on 6 April, noting that he understood that Charles B. Hogg of the FCC had been designated for assignment to Cuba and requesting that he be sent as soon as possible. Hogg arrived in Havana with the equipment on 10 April.

Later in the year, Sterling picked eight more volunteers and notified them on 10 October that they had been selected, but that he could not tell them when they would leave. The men selected were George W. Earnhart for Mexico, John W. Cruise for the Dominican Republic, S. R. Lines for Venezuela, Donald E. Strong for Colombia, W.N. Fellows for Uruguay, Dale B. Dorothy for Peru, and Charles R. Weeks for Ecuador. On 2 November Fellows' assignment was changed to Chile, to free de Bardeleben for other duties in that country, and Paul Means was assigned to Uruguay.[156]

Two factors were responsible for delaying the transfers and the implementation of the program. As of 17 November, the communications equipment had not been delivered to Miami for forwarding to the various U.S. missions, and the CIAA had not yet come up with the funds to pay travel and per diem costs for the FCC personnel. The delay in supply had been caused by a shortage of essential materials used in the manufacture of some of the equipment. The equipment arrived in Miami at the end of November, and after strenuous FCC representations to the CIAA, the State Department, and the American Intelligence Corps (AIC), as the headquarters in Miami had been designated, the engineers were ordered to depart their current duty stations for Washington, D.C., on 3/4 January 1943. After spending four days in Washington and three days in Miami, they were to leave for their duty assignments on 12 January. A final meeting was held in Washington on 7 January to give the engineers a send-off. In addition to the men themselves, the meeting was attended by representatives of the FBI, the State Department, the FCC, the CIAA, and the War Department. The Navy was not represented.[157]

In December MID and the FBI had reached agreement with regard to the operation of the network and the responsibilities of the two agencies. MID was to be responsible for establishment of the network by lending DF and communications equipment to the countries involved; furnishing technical assistance and coordinating the sta-tions involved; and disseminating the information obtained to representatives of the FBI, ONI, and the appropriate agency of the host country. The FBI was to be responsible for taking the most advisable action against clandestine stations after conferring with MID, keeping MID representatives supplied with all-source information regarding clandestine stations, and the transmission of material through controlled stations as requested by MID.[158]

Implementation of the Concept: January 1943 to the War's End

In most of the countries where FCC personnel were sent, only minor difficulties, usually of a technical nature, were encountered. The men sent to Cuba, Chile, and Argentina, however, met with active opposition to their work.

Cuba–Graft and Corruption

During his tour in Cuba, Charles Hogg encountered considerable obstruction from the Director of Cuban Public Radio, Commandante Juan Govea. Govea had been responsible for the organization of an "Auxiliary Corps of Radio Amateurs," who were to patrol the radio spectrum listening for suspicious signals. When Hogg advocated closing down amateur radio communications, Govea registered strong opposition. Up to the time Hogg left Cuba on 11 July 1942, Govea had refused to give him an accurate list of the radio transmitters in Cuba. Even after amateur broadcasting was closed down on 21 July, many transmitters continued to operate, taking advantage of loopholes in the law.

Up to his departure, Hogg had found no evidence of clandestine radio activity. Ambassador Braden interpreted this as meaning that such activity had ceased upon Hogg's publicized arrival, and with this in mind, suggested to the State Department that Hogg be reassigned to Havana for another ninety days. The FCC concurred and Hogg returned to Havana on 12 September.[159]

Upon his return, Hogg determined that Govea was involved in graft, illegal confiscation of equipment, and other questionable practices. More important to Hogg was the discovery that Govea was operating the control transmitter of a net made up of nine unlicensed stations whose operators had unsavory reputations. Apparently Govea was trying to establish his own commercial net for ship-to-shore and paid message operation. Hogg considered any one of the men involved capable of causing damage to the war effort with the proper monetary encouragement.

Ambassador Braden explained to the Foreign Ministry that Govea was using his illicit net to transmit information detrimental to the Allied Nations war effort, and Govea was relieved of his post on 6 November 1942. He continued to receive his salary until April 1943, when the Radio Directorate was combined with Postal Censorship and Cable Censorship under Dr. Eugenio Castillo, who was designated Coordinator of War Information. Castillo, who was directly subordinate to the Chief of the Cuban Police, reorganized all departments, to the benefit of both efficiency and morale.

Hogg had constructed an Adcock-type DF in December 1942 but had been unable to interest Govea or his interim successors in its operation, even though one of those successors, Lieutenant Jose Gata, had attended the FCC course in Laurel. A new U.S. military attaché, Major Charles Youmans, added his backing to Hogg's efforts, and in June 1943 this equipment went into twenty-four-hour operation and became part of the Latin American Direction-Finding Network. After establishing this station, callsign CLQ, Hogg conducted a survey of radio transmitters in Cuba and returned to the United States in October 1943.[160]

Chile–Nazis and Mountains

From the beginning of his tour in Chile, John de Bardeleban was hindered by two factors: the enormous influence wielded by the Nazis in Chilean governmental, military, and police circles; and the topography of Chile. It was evident immediately that local Nazis were keeping close tabs on his movements and activities, to the extent that when he would leave the city for the countryside with his equipment, the agent transmitter would cease operation. As a result, most of his operations were performed undercover with only a very limited number of local officials being informed. At one point, he was smuggled into a private home on the outskirts of Valparaiso and remained there for two months, attempting to get bearings on PYL, the agent station. As it happened, the agent transmitter was in storage for the entire period and was not being used.

The topography of the country created its own set of problems. There were no accurate maps, few good roads, and massive underground deposits of metallic ores that caused unpredictable errors in bearings by either shielding or reflecting target signals. One time, to reach a useful DF site location, it was necessary for de Bardeleben and an associate from the embassy to backpack the DF equipment five miles over three hills that were from 600 to 2,000 feet high. It was then necessary to wait two or three hours, in mid-winter, until transmission began.

De Bardeleban did receive full cooperation from the U.S. embassy and the attachés, although in most cases they were not sure what he was supposed to be doing.[161]

W. N. Fellows was notified on 31 October 1942 to prepare for a six-month TDY to Chile. As a result of the usual problems in getting the CIAA to make arrangements for transportation, Fellows did not arrive on station until January 1943. Sterling felt that a two-week overlap was sufficient for bringing Fellows into the operation in Chile. Fellows was told that it was understood that upon the completion of the communications facility reports and the installation of the technical equipment that had been sent to Chile, the communications and DF facilities would be taken over and operated by AIS personnel assigned to that duty by Colonel Collins.

After that, neither his nor de Bardeleban's presence would be required. Sterling and Fly had the impression that de Bardeleban wanted to return to the United States because of family problems, and ordered him to return home in March 1943. A cable from de Bardeleban on 30 March and a follow-up letter sent the next day, however, contained a request that he remain in Chile on an accompanied tour. He also asked about the possibility of a pay increase and an in-grade pay raise for serving in a foreign assignment. His request was turned down on 5 April.[162]

From this shed at Quilpe, a small town 18 miles east of Valparaiso, a German spy ring in Chile operated a radio transmitter with callsign PYL to send information to the Abwehr radio station in Hamburg.

Argentina—More Nazis

Despite Norman's and Sterling's reservations on sending de Bardeleban abroad again, he and Francis M. McDermott left for Buenos Aires on 4 July 1943. Unfortunately, there was a revolu-

tion in Argentina that day which resulted in the installation of a thoroughly anti-U.S. government. Consequently, there were difficulties in accomplishing the mission.

The clandestine net in Argentina consisted of several terminals, each of which could employ several frequencies and shift among them with ease. This net operated in a country thickly populated with pro-Nazi Germans. The Abwehr, which initially controlled the net, had seen others of its nets in South America closed down by U.S. and local governmental action and wanted to avoid a repeat in Argentina. It appeared that the Abwehr would stop at nothing to guarantee maintenance of their last channel of rapid communication between Argentina and the Fatherland. As a consequence of these circumstances, and the fact that there were large numbers of Argentine nationals working in the U.S. embassy, security was a major problem. Although the original concept of AIS stations was that they would work overtly training local personnel, the station in Buenos Aires appears to have been covert from the start. De Bardeleban and McDermott worked only with the first secretary of the embassy, Hugh Milliard, and one vice consul, Clifton English. Milliard was kept fully aware of all activities and results, but retained no copies of any paperwork shown to him. English appears to have been in charge of administrative details, such as travel pay, per diem, housing, etc., for the team.

The attaché staffs could not be used for support purposes as they were in other South American countries. The naval attaché's office was considered to be particularly insecure, as most of the personnel had been employed by the Argentine shipping companies in peacetime. The problem with the military attaché's office was it was not connected with security. Since the AIS was under Army control, the military attaché, Colonel John Lang, assumed that the Argentine DF station was to be under his control. Lang also believed that any tip coming from his office should be investigated thoroughly. Once administrative channels had been made clear, however, Lang cooperated with de Bardeleban and McDermott.

After six months, the team had determined that it was not possible to locate the clandestine stations with only two DF units operating under the conditions prevailing in Argentina. The stations were moving frequently, in some cases every two or three days; and it was nearly impossible for the DF units to move, communicate, and operate without being spotted. As a result, the team recommended that at least four additional mobile units be provided to continue the search. This would, of course, require additional automobiles, equipment, housing, and personnel. The embassy frowned on this recommendation both because of the increased expense and because of the implied heightening of the team's profile. The latter was particularly important because the Argentinian government was believed to be itching for a chance to pin anything even resembling espionage on the U.S. embassy.

An alternative to the above was to try to arrange to get bearings from the Adcock DFs in Montevideo, Santiago, and Lima. This was considered to be a very weak alternative because the distances over which the bearings would be taken would not permit sufficient accuracy to locate the targets.

Since the embassy was so opposed to the first solution, McDermott thought that the entire project should be held at a standstill pending further developments, particularly possible changes in the attitude of the Argentine government.[163]

Not all of the teams ran into the sort of difficulties that de Bardeleban encountered in Chile and Argentina. Many of the Latin American republics were resolute in their efforts to aid the allied nations. Others had an attitude problem.

Ecuador–Mañana Land

Charles Weeks arrived in Quito on 13 January 1943, and contacted the chargé d'affaires, Alfred T.

Neslen, and the U.S. military attaché, Colonel W. E. Shipp, who arranged a meeting with the Ecuadoran minister of public works, Sr. Alberto Wright.

When Weeks arrived, Chief Radiomen Bradford and Maltz, who had been sent to Ecuador in 1941, were conducting a school in direction finding for local military officers, and seven Ecuadoran officers were standing research and monitoring watches. Bradford and Maltz were also assisting the naval attaché in his investigation of clandestine radio stations. Upon Week's arrival, they were detailed to help him in his work. The Adcock-type DT direction finder which had been left in Ecuador by the U.S. Navy when the war started was housed in an adobe building on the grounds of the Ecuadoran Military College and was being used by Bradford and Maltz in their classes. In addition, one of the DF trucks sent to Ecuador by the Navy in 1940 was on hand with its associated equipment.

The three Americans made numerous trips out of Quito in all directions, performing a series of tests to find a new location for the equipment while the Ecuadoran watch standers took special check bearings as directed by Weeks to check the accuracy of the equipment. Weeks determined that while the present DF site was the best in Quito, the surrounding mountains and the building itself were inducing considerable error in the bearings obtained.[164]

Weeks found that Guayaquil was the ideal location for the DF and so notified AIS, but was told by them that the equipment was to stay in Quito. AIS did, however, provide funds for a circular wooden building to house the equipment. New construction and alterations to the old building for use as an intercept site were completed by 28 April. The equipment, including a shipment from the United States that had arrived on 12 March, was installed and antennas erected by 2 May.

AIS took over physical control, via the U.S. military attaché, as of 26 March 1943. Maltz and Bradford were transferred to the Naval Radio

Station, Chatham, Massachussetts, on 15 March. They were replaced by three U.S. Army personnel, Sergeant Arthur Swarz and Corporals Charles Catrona and Jose Perez. These three, with Navy permission, took custody of the Navy DF equipment. The only Ecuadoran personnel with any background in DF were the military personnel trained by Bradford and Maltz. The Ministry of Public Works official appointed to direct the Ecuadoran personnel, Sr. Alfonso Zabala, was urged to obtain a number of these men to work at the site. The minister of public works, however, pointed out that his appropriation for this work had run out and suggested that the Ministry of Defense take over. This was done. On 11 May eight Ecuadoran Army officers and one Ministry of Communications civilian reported rather unenthusiastically for duty.

Weeks reported that throughout this period he had received little or no aid from Ecuadoran authorities, who seemed to have little interest in the project and little ambition to locate and close clandestine stations in Ecuador.

After having his TDY extended thirty days on 15 April and forty-five days on 15 May, Weeks returned to the United States in July 1943.[166]

Colombia–Everything in Place

The equipment that the U.S. Navy had taken into Colombia had also been left there and in late 1942 was being used by Chief Radioman Everett Fowlkes to train Colombian Army personnel. This equipment was turned over to the military attaché in February 1943. According to the military attaché, writing in November 1942, Captain Roldan of the Colombian Army Air Corps deserved the credit for maintaining the equipment and for continuing to improve the Colombian radio intelligence service.[166]

The Colombian Ministry of War and the U.S. missions in Colombia were anxious to have all of the radio locator equipment in Bogotá because that city was the capital and because it had the only

reliable electrical supply in the country. After his arrival in early January, Donald Strong managed to balance the type DY direction finder so that the minima were acceptable. The original site chosen for installation of the DF was Techo, six miles west of Bogotá, but in March it was decided to construct an airfield on that site.

Strong's tour of duty was extended in April, and he managed to find an excellent site for the DF, complete with a ten-room house. On 12 April he predicted that his job would be completed by 1 May. However, by 26 April there had been an abortive coup d'état, official visits by (among others) U.S. vice president Henry Wallace, and Holy Week. So the minister of war did not get around to signing the lease. Strong's tour was extended again on 14 May, and he brought the monitoring station into active operation on 13 June. He left for the United States five or six days later.[167]

Brazil–Full Cooperation

The FCC officer selected for duty in Brazil was Robert D. Linx, monitoring officer at Austin, Texas, who was ordered to Miami in March 1942, at the same time as de Bardeleben. He arrived in Rio on 20 March, and after surveying the situation, requested additional equipment, including a complete automobile DF assembly. His primary job was to help Brazil organize a radio monitoring service. Within a month of his arrival, the Brazilians had been persuaded to establish six monitoring posts along the coast, with more to come. Linx spent the first two weeks of May preparing the Rio de Janeiro station of the service, which was titled Posto Radio Escuto (PRE) and headed by Ezequiel Martims. As of 10 May there were sixty-three cases on file at PRE RIO, most of them clandestine. Linx noted that it had been necessary to instruct the six secondary stations in their duties by mail, a task that was made doubly hard because the average Brazilian technician had to be given a reason for everything he did. By the end of the month, Linx was able to report to Theodore A. Xanthaki at the U.S. embassy that the first phase of the operation was complete. Seven stations were in operation and fully supplied, and an Adcock DF was under construction. Linx estimated that as soon as these were installed and he had the mobile DF he had ordered, most of the known clandestine stations could be located. In August he added the mobile DF to the operation.[168]

At this point, PRE's seven stations (Rio de Janeiro, Sao Paulo, Porto Alegro, Belo Horizonte, Natal, Recife, and Belem) employed sixty-three first-class operators and seven chief operators. Each PRE station was operating twenty-four hours a day, with four operators on duty at PRE RIO and two each at each of the subordinate stations during the heavy traffic hours of 2100-0300Z. PRE RIO was able to issue instructions to the other stations by radio, transmitting either in the clear or using a five-letter code to which only the chief operators had access. Three additional secondary stations were planned, to be located at Manaus, Baia, and between Natal and Belem. PRE RIO's mobile unit was received from the United States and was ready for operation by the end of July. Also in July, the Ministry of Aviation turned over its Rio radio post to PRE, where it received the designation PRE MAE. The same month, Lieutenant Commander A. Pinheiro de Andrade, who was retired from the Brazilian Navy, was added to the staff as a crypt-analyst.[169]

The Brazilians were extremely proud of the PRE. The FBI's Jack West called it the best in South America. At the end of July, Major Landry Salles Goncalves, the director-general of Posts and Telegraphs, and Major Lauro Medeiros, the director of the Brazilian Telegraph System, spoke to the U.S. ambassador about Linx, praising him fulsomely and referring to him as the "Father of the Brazilian Monitoring Service."[170]

The Adcocks were completed in September and placed in Rio (outside the city), Porto Allegro. Belem, Recife, and Campo Grande. PRE had been asked (it is not clear by whom) to cooperate with the British DF system in Africa. In his report on

this, Linx stated that "the party in charge of this system is an employee of the Marconi Company in Brazil." Since Linx had information that the head of the Marconi Company in Brazil was a well-known Fascist, he intended to have a complete investigation made before taking action on the request. Since he did not mention the subject again, it may be assumed that the British net passed the security investigation.[171]

Linx had been due to return to the United States in August 1942, but the U.S. ambassador strongly opposed moving him until PRE was fully viable. Linx was extended for another six months. In the end, he remained in Brazil until November 1945. At that point there seemingly was no one left in FCC or State who remembered how he had been sent to Brazil or how he was to be returned home. When he was notified that FCC had no place for him because of the high grade he had attained, he transferred to the State Department to become communications attaché in Rio de Janeiro.[172]

The AIS Takes Over

The tours of the other men sent to Latin America were considerably less eventful; and the attitudes of the countries involved fell somewhere in between Chile and Argentina, on the one hand, and Brazil, on the other. Earnhart and Crews returned home after ninety days, and Means and Dorothy after 120 days, their tasks completed. Lines was extended until August 1942 and then returned. Upon the conclusion of their tours, de Bardeleben, Crews, Fellows, Hogg, Linx, and Strong received letters of commendation from the State Department for their work in Latin America.[173]

As the men returned home, the stations were taken over by either local military personnel, AIS personnel, or some combination of the two. In 1943 or 1944, de Bardeleben and McDermott visited the stations in Chile and Uruguay, respectively. What they found does not seem to have been very encouraging. According to de Bardeleben, the U.S. Army operators at the Chilean site were incompetent and unable to copy Morse code at reasonable speeds. The Chilean Air Force operators were superior to the U.S. operators, who were supposed to be instructing the Chileans in DF operations and intercept. Transmissions on the Argentine clandestine net were too fast for the U.S. operators to copy.

> *The U.S. operators in Chile lacked coordination from Miami and spent most of their time chatting on their radio circuits or with each other about the living conditions and what a hard life they had. They monitored very little and left most of the work for the local operators, who had no training in signal recognition at all. Even the Army operators appeared to have complete faith in the call letters used and if they sounded legal made no other attempt to copy the traffic. In short, they didn't recognize legal from clandestine stations when heard, and had no radio background or knowledge. They had no idea at all of radio fundamentals and frequency differences from day to night. In addition, there was no officer at the Adcock, so the men worked only when they felt like it.[174]*

McDermott found similar conditions in Uruguay and made the additional comment that

> *the inefficiency and poor administration of the South American Adcock system demands that they be eliminated from participation in this case. Particularly in view of the high degree of security required.[175]*

The Army tried to turn the Bogotá, Quito, and Montevideo intercept and DF sites over to the Coast Guard, since most of their operation had been for the benefit of the Coast Guard. The Army also wanted the Coast Guard to assume control of the hemisphere radio direction finding net.[176]

The hemisphere network, controlled by WVSM, consisted of Station HKU3, Bogotá, Colombia, manned by six enlisted men of the 2nd Signal Service Battalion; Station HC1YZ, Quito. Ecuador, manned by five enlisted men of the 2nd Signal Service Battalion, working in conjunction with six or seven natives; Station CXW, Montevideo, Uruguay, manned by six enlisted men of the 2nd Signal Service Battalion, assisted by eight or nine natives; Station CBA2, Quintero, Chile, manned by eight men from the United States Coast Guard and six or eight men from the Chilean Air Force; Station OBC, Callao, Peru, manned by six United States Coast Guardsmen and ten members of the Peruvian Navy; Station HIQG, Ciudad Trujillo, Dominican Republic, manned by six United States Coast Guardsmen and two or three members of the Dominican Republic Army; Station XBTW, Merida, Yucatan, Mexico, manned by about twelve men from the Mexican Army; Station WL2, Rio Hato, Panama Canal Zone, until recently operated by a detachment of the 120th Signal Radio Intelligence Company, and thereafter by local United States Army units under Colonel Tatom; Station CLQ, Havana, Cuba, manned by Cuban military, naval, and civilian personnel; and Station PPG, Posto Radio Escuta, which was a Brazilian radio intelligence network operated in its entirety by the Brazilian Department of Post and Telegraphs.[177]

A comment made by the U.S. naval attaché in Bogotá could serve as a characterization of most of the AIS DF operation, Brazil always excluded:

> *The operation in Colombia was never successful, because of the lack of Colombian Government cooperation. There is no reason to believe that it would be successful in the future, because there is no reason to believe that the Colombians will cooperate in the future. The reasons for the latter statement are (a) the belief that German submarine warfare in the Caribbean is a thing of the past and therefore Colombia is*

under no direct threat from the Axis; (b) Captain Alvaro ROLDAN, would undoubtedly again be in charge; and (c) Colonel Arturo LEMA Posada, Director-General of the Colombian Air Force, is less effective and cooperative than was Colonel Ernesto BUENA VENTURA, who was in charge in 1940 but was relieved by LEMA in February 1942. The military attaché would like to turn everything over to the naval attaché as of January 1945; but the naval attaché does not have radio technical personnel under his command.[178]

Disposition of the AIS Net

As of 28 December 1944, the U.S. naval attaché, Montevideo, had taken responsibility for the clandestine intercept and DF station there. The Cuban portion of the DF system was destroyed by a hurricane in the autumn of 1944. In February 1945, in answer to a query from the secretary of state about whether the Cuban site was to be rebuilt, Admiral Ralph Bard, the assistant secretary of the navy, replied that the network was adequate for full coverage of clandestine radio in Latin America and should be maintained until it was no longer useful. However, no increase in personnel or equipment would be profitable. Therefore, if the Colombians did not want to provide personnel to work the station in Bogotá, the station could be closed down, and there was no need to rebuild the Cuban station. At this time there were no USCG operators in Bogotá, Montevideo, or Merida.[179]

The last of the elements of the network to survive was the PRE, since it had never been under U.S. government control. On 18 January 1946, however, the secretary of the navy informed the secretary of state that

The Navy Department has no interest in the continuation, by Brazilian authorities, of the monitoring in Brazil of clandestine radio stations. . . .

. . .In view of the possibility that the U.S. Coast Guard may be interested in the Brazilian monitoring, it is suggested that the question of its continuation be referred to the Secretary of the Treasury, under whom that service now operates.[180]

Conclusion

Did the Axis clandestine effort in the Western Hemisphere have any effect on the conduct of the war? Probably not. It appears that most of the intelligence passed to Germany was of little significance. Station AOR, run by the FBI, probably passed more useful, valid intelligence to the Germans than all the rest of the German nets put together, and according to the Coast Guard, was responsible for the sinking of several Allied ships. But this was a minor contribution to the Battle of the Atlantic.

The answer to the question, "Did the U.S. cryptanalytic effort against the Axis spies have any effect on the conduct of the war?" is also, "probably not." But because most clandestine communications operations are more alike than they are different, it was a useful exercise that provided valuable experience for the postwar years.

Notes

1. Barbara W. Tuchman, *The Zimmermann Telegram* (New York: Viking Press), 1958.

2. "Axis Aspirations through South America," FBI monograph (April 1942).

3. David Kahn, *Hitler's Spies* (New York: MacMillan, 1978), 32, 51, 224.

4. Ibid., 225.

5. Ibid., 229, 231-32.

6. GC&CS publication, *Amt Auslandsnachrichten and Abwehr*, as excerpted in COL Alfred McCormack's report on his trip to London, May-June 1943, 51; Lauren Paine, *German Military Intelligence in World War II:*

The Abwehr (New York: Stein and Day, 1984), 11-13; and Ladislas Farago, *The Game of the Foxes* (New York: David McKay, 1971), 1.

7. McCormack Trip Report, 53-55, "Epitome of the German Intelligence Service," SHAEF, Counter-Intelligence War Room (April 1946; and Kahn, *Hitler's Spies*, 243-48).

8. McCormack Trip Report, 58; Kahn, *Hitler's Spies*, 231-32; and "Epitome of the German Intelligence Services."

9. "Epitome of the German Intelligence Services."

10. Ibid.

11. McCormack's Trip Report, 1-2.

12. The Interrogation of Hedwig Elisabeth Weigelmayer Sommer, FBI File No. 65-118 (10 May 1945), 15.

13. Ibid., 15-16; "Latin America: Clandestine Radio Stations Utilized by the German Espionage System," an FBI report dated February 1942; and "Radio 'CEL'– Albrecht Gustav Engela, WAS: et al–Brazil Espionage," 3-8. This 194-page document describing the entire operations of the CELALD espionage net is of unknown authorship, but was possibly originated by OP-20-GL.

14. "Radio CEL," 4.

15. FBI Report of February 1942.

16. Sommer interrogation, 21.

17. Ibid., 24.

18. FBI Report of February 1942.

19. Ibid; and FBI memorandum, "Individuals Operating in Connection with Clandestine Radio Station PYL, Valparaiso" (10 March 1942).

20. Ibid., 27, 28; and a 22 March 1944 message from Argentina to Berlin (CG4-3895).

21. Sommer interrogation, 29; and Op-20-GI-A memorandum, "The JOLLE Operation" (25 August 1944).

22. Sommer interrogation, 26; OP-20-GI-A memorandum of 25 August 1944; letter from Vice Chief of Naval Operations, "Sub Contact in Argentina" (16 September 1943); and LUNA's 22 March 1944 message to Berlin (CG4-3891).

23. Berlin's 30 March 1944 message to Argentina (CG4-4014).

24. Extract from BAD Summary #117, date unknown, detailing information received from four prisoners of war who had served aboard *Passim*; and OP-20-GI-A's 25 August 1944.

25. Stanley E. Hilton, *Hitler's Secret War in South America, 1939-1946* (Baton Rouge: Louisiana State University Press, 1981), 288-93.

26. Ibid., 293-303; and OP-20-GI-A memorandum to F-21 (27 July 1944).

27. OP-20-GI-A memorandum of 25 August 1944.

28. 10 May 1944 mesaage from Berlin to Argentina (CG4-4579); Argentina's 24 May 1944 (CG4-????), and 3 June 1944 (CG4-4938); and Hilton, *Hitler's Secret War in South America, 1939-1945*, 293.

29. Berlin's 6 June 1944 (CG4-4929); Argentina's 9 June 1944 (CG4-4964-A); and Berlin's 18 June 1944 (CG4-4987).

30. Berlin's 15 June 1944 to Franczok, quoted in R.I. Summary, Part I (21 June 1944).

31. Argentina's 21 June 1944 to *Passim* (CG4-5006-A); *Passim's*, 21 June 1944 to Argentina (CG4-5007-A); Argentina's 23 June 1944 to *Passim* (CG4-5050-A); and Argentina's 4 July 1944 to Berlin (CG4-5134).

32. Sommer interrogation, 31-32.

33. Ibid., 33; BAD Summary #117 of POW Interrogation; and Intelligence Summary–Blue (ISB), No. 10 (10 October 1944), and No. 12 (24 October 1944). (The Intelligence Summary–Blue was an all-source intelligence report, apparently British, issued approximately weekly from 7 July 1944 to 21 December 1945.)

34. CDR L.T. Jones's 7 September 1944 memorandum to OP-20-G.

35. CG3-1411 (1 July 1943); CG3-2125 (7 October 1945); CG3-2364 (1 November 1943); and CG4-3065 (17 January 1944).

36. Memorandum from Carl B. Spaeth (Special Assistant to Spruille Braden) to Dean Acheson, "The Argentine Project" (17 January 1946).

37. Letter from ADM D. C. Ramsey to Carl B. Spaeth (22 January 1946); Spaeth's 17 January 1946 to Acheson; and memorandum from CAPT W. R. Smedburg III to ADM Stone, "U.S. State Department Case against Argentina" (7 February 1946).

38. "Organizational Development of the Naval Security Group," CAPT J. S. Holtwick, Jr., USN (Ret.), 1-2.

39. Ibid., 2.

40. Ibid., 3.

41. Ibid.

42. Ibid., 4.

43. Ibid., 4-6.

44. "Military Study: Communications Intelligence Research Activities," by LT Joseph N. Wenger, USN (30 June 1937), 9-12, 18, 22.

45. Holtwick, Development of NSG, 5.

46. "History of OP-20-GU (Coast Guard Unit of NCA)" (16 October 1943), 1-2.

47. Ibid., 3; and a memorandum for the Secretary of the Treasury from RADM R. R. Waesche, Commandant, USCG (16 November 1938).

48. Memorandum from LT Frank E. Pollio to the Chief Personnel Officer (26 March 1937), 2-5; and "History of OP-20-GU," 10.

49. Memorandum from CDR J. F. Farley, USCG, to CDR John R. Redman, ONC (6 March 1942).

50. Ibid.

51. Memorandum from CDR L. T. Jones (USCG) to OP-20-G, "Clandestine Radio Intelligence" (7 September 1944) "History of OP-20-GU" (16 October 1943), 2.

52. Memorandum from LCDR Pollio and LT Jones to CAPT J. W. Chalker, Commandant, USCG (28 October 1940).

53. Memorandum from CDR L. T. Jones to OP-20-G (7 September 1944).

54. "History of OP-20-GU," 2, 3; Executive memoranda of 26 June 1939 and unknown date in 1939.

55. Memoranda from CDR Farley to FCC Chief Engineer Jett (23 July 1940); and to FCC Chairman Fly (21 October 1940).

56. "The Radio Intelligence Division of the Federal Communications Commission" (August 1943), 9-10. (This rather self-serving report was issued by the FCC in answer to the charges made by the House Committee to investigate the Federal Communications Commission, better known as the Cox Committee.)

57. Hoover's letters to Fly on 7 Sep, 11 October, and 23 December 1940; and Fly's letters to Hoover on 7 December 1940 and 18 January 1941.

58. Hoover's letters to Fly on 14 and 23 December 1940, and 8 February, 21 February, 28 February, 5 March, 28 April, and 30 April 1941; and letters from RADM L. C. Covell, Assistant Commandant, USCG, to T. J. Slowie, Secretary of the FCC. on 24 April and 2 May 1941.

59. Memorandum to the Defense Communications Board from E. K. Jett, Chairman of the Coordinating Committee (18 January 1941), with attachments: "Proposed Memorandum for the President from the Defense Communications Board" and the FCC's "Justification for Estimate of Additional Funds . . ."; and letter from the FCC to the DNC (2 Auguat 1941).

60. Hearings, Independent Offices Appropriations Bill, 1941, 893, 903-904, and 931.

61. F. H. Hinsley, *British Intelligence in World War II*, Vol. 1 (London: HMSO, 1979), 20.

62. Ibid., 22-23.

63. LCDR L. A. Griffiths, RNVR, *GC&CS Secret Service SIGINT*, Vol. I, "Organization and Evolution of British Secret Service SIGINT," 20-27.

64. Ibid., 5.

65. lbid., 6-11.

66. Ibid., 13-16.

67. lbid., 16-18.

68. Ibid., 18-22.

69. Ibid., 29, 37-98 passim; and MacCormack Trip Report, 1-2.

70. Ibid., 30-45 and "Report by the Chief, Training Division, to the Director, Armed Forces Security Agency, on Clandestine Communications" (7 January 1952), 10-11.

71. Memorandum from Franklin D. Roosevelt (26 June 1939).

72. Memorandum from Franklin D. Roosevelt (1939).

73. Letter from RADM T. S. Wilkinson to A. A. Berle (28 March 1942). The story of the operations of the Brazilian network and its fate is covered fully in Hilton's *Hitler's Secret War in South America, 1939-1945*.

74. Wilkinson letter to Berle.

75. Memorandum from CDR John R. Redman to the DNI and the DNC, "Radio Intelligence Activities with Respect to Clandestine Radio Stations," 3 April 1942; and letter from Gen Strong to A. A. Berle, 3 April 1942.

76. Redman memorandum to DNI and DNC.

77. Redman memorandum to DNI and DNC.

78. Memorandum from J. B. W. Waller, Office of tbe CNO, to CDR Redman and LCDR Kramer, "Conference re Radio Intercepts" (10 April 1942); "Report of

Subcommittee of the Interdepartmental Intelligence Conference Appointed to Explore the Cryptanalytic Work of the War Department, Navy Department, and Federal Bureau of Investigation" (23 April 1942); and "Report of Conference Appointed to Study Processing and Dissemination of Radio Intelligence" (25 May 1942).

79. Memorandum from ADM Wilkinson to the JCS, "Limitation of Cryptanalytic Activities" (18 June 1942).

80. 'Report of Conference Appointed to Study Allocation of Cryptanalysis" (30 June 1942).

81. JCS memorandum to the President (6 July 1942); White House memorandum to the Director of the Budget (8 July 1942); memorandum from W.O. Hall to B. L. Gladieux (16 July 1942); letter from John H. Sorrells, Deputy Director of Office of Censorship, to the Director of the Budget (12 August 1942); and memorandum from the Assistant Director of the Budget to the President (1 September 1942).

82. Letters from Assistant Secretary of State A. A. Berle to Chairman Fly on 22 October 1940 and 10 April 1941; from Assistant Secretary of State Breckenridge Long to Chairman Fly on 6 November 1940 and 29 January and 12 May 1941; from Chairman Fly to the DNC (16 July 1940); and from CAPT E. C. Raguet, Acting DNC, to the FCC (19 August 1940).

83. "History of OP-20.GU," 5-6.

84. Letter from H. Morgenthau, Secretary of the Treasury, to James Forrestal, Secretary of the Navy (10 November 1941); Forrestal's reply (3 December 1941); memorandum from LCDR Alwin D. Kramer to OP-20-G, "Cryptanalysis: FBI Activities and Liaison with the British" (8 June 1942); "Report of Conference to Study Allocation of Cryptanalysis" (30 June 1942); and "History of OP-20GU," 3, 7; memorandum from the Commandant, USCG, to LCDR L. T. Jones, "Change in Location of Communications Intelligence Section," 4 February 1943; and memorandum from the Chief Communications Officer, USCG, to DNC (4 February 1943).

85. Memorandum from D. M. Stanier to OP-20-G. "Activities of Clandestine South American Stations" (16 February 1942); and memoranda from Officer in Charge, Station "U," to CNO, "Caribbean High-Frequency Direction Finder Net–Clandestine Stations," 1, 9, 14, and 21 February 1942, among others.

86. Memorandum to LCDR Cross, "Clandestine Coverage–Conference with Lieutenant Commander Jones" (12 March 1942).

87. Telephone call from ADM Leigh Noyes, DNC, to E. K. Jett (12 July 1940), quoted in scrapbook notes included in the Papers of George Sterling, Box 11, RG173, FRC, Suitland, Maryland; and letter from DNC to Chairman Fly (7 August 1940).

88. Scrapbook notes; and letter from CAPT E. C. Raguet, Acting DNC, to Chairman Fly (19 August 1940).

89. Scrapbook notes; and letter from DNC to Chairman Fly (17 September 1940).

90. Scrapbook notes; and memorandum from OP-20-G to OP-20 (9 December 1940).

91. Scrapbook notes.

92. Memorandum from CAPT J. F. Farley (USCG) to CDR J. R. Redman (USN) (28 March 1942), 1.

93. Ibid., 2-3.

94. Memorandum from CDR L.T. Chalker, USCG, Acting Assistant Commandant, to the Commander, New York District, "Headquarters Monitoring Assignment Group 2-A" (13 September 1941).

96. "History of OP-20-GU," 5-6, 11; memorandum from CDR Jones to OP-20-G (7 September 1944); memorandum from OP-20-G to DNI, "Request of Claude G. Bowers for Certain Decoded Material" (24 September 1942).

96. Memorandum from LT L.T. Jones to Herbert B. Gaston, Assistant Secretary of the Treasury, "Communications of German Agents in the United States and Other Points in the Western Hemisphere" (23 May 1941); and memorandum from CDR Jones to OP-20-G (7 September 1944), 2-3; and memorandum from J. N. Wenger to OP-20-G (28 May 1943); and "Agreement Between FBI, MID, and ONI for the Operation of a Network to Locate Clandestine Radio Stations in Latin America, and the Action to Be Taken upon the Information Derived Therefrom," signed by MGEN George V. Strong, RADM H. C. Train, and J. Edgar Hoover (6 February 1943).

97. Memorandum from D. M. Stanier to OP-20-G (16 February 1942); "History of OP-20-GU," 4; and memorandum from S. N. Wilson to LCDR Cross, "Suggestion by LCDR Jones, USCG, that the Undersigned Attend

Conferences on Clandestine Intercept Operations" (28 January 1943).

98. Memorandum from CDR Jones to OP-20-G (7 September 1944), 3.

99. Ibid.

100. Ibid., 3-4.

101. Ibid.

102. Memorandum from CDR Jones to OP-20-G (7 September 1944); memorandum from CAPT E. B. Stone, OP-20-G, to COL Carter W. Clarke, "German Clandestine Traffic" (6 February 1943); Cable CXG-358 from the Chief of the Secret Service (CSS) to CAPT Hastings, RN (11 February 1943); and his reply, Cable CXG-898, of 13 February 1943; and memorandum from OP-20-G to ADM Schuirmann, "Communication Intelligence — Dissemination of Clandestine Information to FBI" (20 October 1943).

103. Letter from J. E. Hoover to DNI (8December 1943).

104. Letter from RADM R. E. Schuirmann, DNI, to J. E. Hoover (20 December 1943).

105. "History of Espionage T/A Study" undated, 1-5.

106. "History of Espionage T/A Study," 8-9 and "History of Special German Diplomatic Net" (1 June 1943), 24-25.

107. "Report on Establishment of Radio Intelligence Center," undated. This document was signed by LTC Laurence H. Smith, Assistant Signal Officer, WDC; CDR F. E. Venzel, Jr., District Communications Officer, Twelfth Naval District; and George E. Sterling, Chief, NDO.

108. Transcript of telephone conversation between General DeWitt and COL Raymond (14 January 1942).

109. File #300.6 WTO(Sig). Headquarter. Western Defense Command and Fourth Army, undated; letter from the Adjutant General's Office to the Commanding General, Field Forces, and the Commanding General, Western Defense Command, "Joint Radio Intelligence Center" (7 February 1942); letter from the Assistant Adjutant General, Western Defense Command and Fourth Army, to the Chief Signal Officer, "Transfer of Funds for Radio Intelligence Center" undated, and File #676.3 (Sig), Headquarters WDC, undated.

110. Memorandum from CDR Safford to CAPT Schuirmann, "Direction Finders for South American Countries" (17 June 1940); Enclosure "A" to CNO's memorandum to Commandant, Fifteenth Naval District, "Clandestine Radio Activities in South American Countries" (16 July 1940); Safford's memoranda to Schuirmann, "Direction Finders for South American Countries (19 and 26 June 1940); and OP-20-G memorandum for file, "Radio Direction Finder Unit in Colombia" (21 August 1941).

111. State Department message no. 179 from the U.S. Ambassador, Bogotá (3 July 1940).

112. Safford memorandum to Schuirmann, "Direction Finders for South American Countries" (6 July 1940); and OP-20-G memorandum for file (21 August 1941).

113. CNO memoranda to Bureau of Ships, "Mobile Direction Finding Equipment" (16 July 1940); to the Commandant, USCG. "Request for Coast Guard Equipment" (16 July 1940); and to the Commandant, Fifteenth Naval District, "Clandestine Radio Activities in South American Countries" (19 July 1940).

114. Memorandum from Commandant, Fifteenth Naval District, to CNO, "Clandestine Radio Activities in South American Countries" (17 August 1940); memorandum from CNO to Bureau of Ships, "Naval Radio Direction Finder Statton Toro Point, Canal Zone–Service Discontinued" (26 September 1940); and CNO's memorandum to the Chief. Bureau of Navigation, "Model DY Direction Finder to Be Established at Farfan Radio Station" (31 December 1940).

115. Memorandum from LCDR McElroy to CNO, "Clandestine Radio Activities in South American Countries (16 August 1940).

116. Memorandum from LCDR E. H. Gardner. OP-20-GX, to CDR Ihrig (20 August 1940), concerning the shipment of radio trucks; memorandum from Atkins and Warren to LCDR Gardner, "Report of Conditions in Colombia, S. A." (8 October 1940); and memorandum from LCDR S. A. Greenleaf, OP-20-GX to McElroy (14 October 1940). (LCDR Gardner had left OP-20-GX on 1 October.)

117. Memoranda from McElroy to CNO, "Clandestine Radio Stations in Colombia" (26 October 1940); and to LCDR Greenleaf (1 November 1940); and from Greenleaf to McElroy (3 December 1940); and Telegram No. 8 from the U.S. Legation at Quito to State Department (12 January 1941).

118. Memorandum from CNO to Commandant, Fifteenth Naval District, "Clandestine Radio Station in South American Countries" (3 January 1941); and memorandum from CAPT Schuirmann to the Undersecretary of State (3 January 1940) (*sic*).

119. Intelligence Report 4-41 from the U.S. Naval Attaché, Quito (17 January 1941); memorandum from Commander, Special Service Squadron. to CNO, "Ecuador: Radio Intelligence Reports re Clandestine Radio Activities in South American Countries" (16 August 1940); and memorandum from CNO to Commandant, Fifteenth Naval District, "Clandestine Radio Activities in South American Countries" (17 February 1941).

120. Memorandum from LTJG J. E. Johnson. Fifteenth Naval District to LCDR S. A. Greenleaf (24 January 1941); OP-16-F-7 memorandum to OP-16-F. "DIF Details in Ecuador and Colombia" (215 January 1941);OP.20.G memorandum to CAPl' Schuirmann. "U.S. Naval Direction Finders and U.S. Navy Radio Operators in Ecuador" (27 January 1941); Cable from ALUSNA Quito to COMFIFTEEN (27 January 1941); and Navy Department Intelligence Report 61.41, from the U.S. Naval Attaché, Quito (4 March 1941).

121. Memorandum from Commandant. Fifteenth Naval District. to CNO. "Clandestine Radio in South America" (5 February 1941).

122. Ibid.; memorandum from Safford to Op-20-A (6 February 1941); Navy Department Intelligence Report 61-41; State Department Message No. 9 from the American Legation, Quito (1 March 1941); memorandum from Safford to the Director, Central Division, 'Navy Direction Finder Unit in Ecuador" (8 March 1941), which mentions the various recommendations made; and memorandum from Safford to CDR McCon, Bureau of Navigation, "Transfer of Enlisted Personnel" (4 April 1941).

123. Memorandum from the Chief, U.S. Naval Mission to Ecuador, to the CNO, "Replacement as Instructors, Operation Navy Roger Dog Fox Equipment in Ecuador; Recommendations for" (11 August 1941); and memorandum from DNC to Director, Central Division, same subject (1 October 1941).

124. OP-16-F-7 memorandum to OP-I6-F (25 January 1941); letter from J. Edgar Hoover to Adolf A. Berle (1 February 1941); OP-20-G memorandum for DNI, "Clandestine Radio in Colombia," serial 043020,

undated; letter from DNI to Hoover (11 June 1941) (drafted by COR. Safford); and McElroy memorandum to Ambassador Spruille Braden, "Clandestine Radio in Colombia" (11 March 1941).

125. Memorandum from OP-20-G to Bureau of Navigation (4 April 1941); and memorandum from the U.S. Naval Attaché, Bogotá, to DNI, "Disorderly Conduct of Radioman 1cl. Jones Atkins, Jr., USNR" (29 May 1941).

126. OP-20-G memorandum for file, "Radio Direction Finder Unit in Colombia" (21 Ausust 1941).

127. Ibid.; State Department Dispatch No. 342 from the U.S. Ambassador, Bogotá (11 August 1941); and a letter from the Secretary of the Navy to the Secretary of State (23 Ausust 1941).

128. Memorandum from CRMs Cullen and Fowlkes to CNO, "Report on Activities in Connection with Instruction and Maintenance of Special Radio D/F Equipment" (27 October 1941); and memorandum from CNO to Naval Attaché, Bogotá, "Radio Direction Finder Operations in Colombia" (23 December 1941).

129. Memorandum from McElroy to Greenleaf November 1940); and Greenleaf's answer (3 December 1940).

130. McElroy memorandum to Greenleaf (12 December 1940).

131. Memorandum from DNC to Director, Central Division, "Radiomen for Duty as Instructors in Direction Finding Operation in Colombia and Ecuador" (23 August 1941); and letter from Greenacre to Safford (13 October 1941).

132. Memorandum from the Senior Member, Naval Radio DF Unit, Quito, Ecuador, to CNO, "Report for October, 1941" (31 October 1941).

133. Memorandum from DNC to Director, Central Division, "Radio Direction Finder Operations in Ecuador" (2 December 1941); and memorandum from Senior Member, Ecuadoran Direction Finder Unit, to CNO, "Report for November, 1941" (2 December 1941).

134. Letter from Safford to Greenacre (17 December 1941); and memorandum from Safford to CDR C. J. Maguire, OP-13 (25 January 1942).

135. State Department Telegram No. 110 from the U.S. Delegation in San Jose (5 September 1940); and letter from Dudley G. Dwyre, Chargé d' Affaires ad interim, to the Secretary of State, "Renewal of Request of

the Costa Rican Government for Assistance in Detecting Illicit and Clandestine Radio Broadcasting Stations Operations in Costa Rica" (13 May 1941). With regard to the supplying of loop-type antennas, CDR Safford, in a memorandum to tbe OIC, Radio Division, Bureau of Ships, on 26 October 1940, said that "the President [had] virtually promised to provide one of these equipments to Costa Rica."

136. Intelligence Report #4-41; and letter from the Navy Department to the State Department (22 October 1941).

137. Cf. memorandum from Commandant, Fifteenth Naval District, to CNO, "Clandestine Radio Station K5BT or HP5BT, Panama City, Republic of Panama" (27 March 1941); 30 September 1941 Intelligence Report, unnumbered, from the U.S. Naval Attaché, Santiago, Chile; and letter from the U.S. Vice-Consul, Valdevia, Chile, to the U.S. Ambassador, Santiago (24 December 1941).

138. *History of American Intelligence Service* (14 February 1946), unpaginated chapter on the Communications Branch.

139. Ibid., 1.

140. "Suppression of Clandestine Radio Stations in the Other American Republics" (31 December 1941). This paper was dictated by George Sterling of the FCC from the State Department's minutes. Attending the meeting were RADM S. C. Hooper and COL J. W. Thomason (USMC) for the Navy Department; MAJ Wesley Guest (USA) for the War Department; Philip F. Siling and George Sterling for the FCC; and a six-man delegation from State Department: Thomas Burke, Francis X. de Wolfe, H. B. Otterman, W. Handley. J. R. Toop, and Mr. (fnu) Halle.

141. Memorandum from E. K. Jett, FCC Chief Engineer, to the Chairman, FCC, "Work Performed by Intercept Unit of the NDO Section" (5 January 1942); memorandum from D. M. Stoner to OP-20-G (16 February 1942); memorandum from George Sterling to Jett, "Assistance Rendered the Federal Bureau of Investigation in the Deciphering of Messages Intercepted from Enemy Espionage Stations" (21 Jnly 1943); and an undated FCC paper, apparently written in January 1942, listing the traffic desired by other agencies.

142. Memorandum from RADM S. C. Hooper to Thomas Burke, Chief, Division of International Communications, State Department, "Technical Requirements of Equipment Necessary for South and Central American Countries to Locate Clandestine Radio Transmitters" (I) January 1942).

143. Memorandum from LCDR C. W. Welker to LCDR F .C. S. Jordan (2 January 1942); and a comment, attached to the Hooper-Burke memorandum of 5 January, signed by LTC J. D. O'Connell, M-7-D-9, U.S. Army Signal Corps, on 28 January 1942.

144. Memorandum from S. W. Norman to J. W. Handley of State Department (25 February 1942).

145. Memorandum from ADM Hooper to BG Frank E. Stoner, Chief, Army Communications Branch, OCSigO, "Location of Clandestine Radio Stations in South and Central America" (5 March 1942).

146. Ibid. and attached note from COL W. T. Guest, Chief, Army Communications Branch.

147. "Report of the Technical Committee Appointed on March 11, 1942, to Recommend Equipment and Technical Procedures Relative to the Enlarged Inter-American Radio Surveillance Program;" State Department Memorandum of Conversation., "Detection of Clandestine Operation of Radio Stations in the Other American Republics" (12 March 1942); memorandum from MAJ T. L. Bartlett (USAAC) to COL A.W. Memner, Director of Communications, USAAC, "Operation of Clandestine Radio Stations in Central and South America" (12 March 1942); and "Meeting in Burke's Office Pursuant to Provisions of Resolution XL of the Rio Conference (Elimination of Clandestine Stations)" (19 March 1942). Attending the 19 March meeting were MAJ T. L. Bartlet (USAAC). MAJ Hayes. and CPT B.N. Massengale, MIS, for the War Department; RADM Hooper. LCDR Jordan. LCDR Welker, and LCDR Fowler for the Navy Department; Messrs. J. R. Troop, F. B. Lyon, J. D. Handley. Thomas Burke, and Francis de Wolfe for State Department; Messrs. Dudley B. Bonsell and John W. G. Ogilvie for the Office of the Coordinator of Inter-American Affairs; and Mr. Norman for the FCC.

148. Memorandum of the meeting on 22 May 1942; State Department memorandum to all American diplomatic officers in the other American republics, "Training Course in the Technical Procedures of Radio Detection and Monitoring" (1 April 1942); and ADM Hooper's "Memorandum for the Army and Navy Representatives

Considering the Question of Suppression of Clandestine Radio Stations in Latin America" (7 May 1942).

149. "Minutes of Informal Meeting on the Subject of the Central and South American Clandestine Radio Situation" (10 April 1942).

150. State Department memorandum of 1 April 1942; Memorandum of Meeting (22 May 1942); and Jett's reply to Sterling (23 May 1942). The following attended the 22 May meeting: VADM A. W. Johnson, Inter-American Defense Board; MAJ T. L. Bartlett (USAAC), MAJ R. E. Schukraft (Signal Corps), and CPT W. E. Plummer (Signal Corps) for the War Department; RADM S. C. Hooper, LCDR F. C. B. Jordan, LTJG Alonso Laidlaw. and ENS Richard Wheeler for the Navy; P. F. Siling and A. W. Norman for the FCC; Elliott S. Hanson and Townsend Munson for the CIAA; and J.R. Troop, J. D. Handley, Thomas Burke, F. C. de Wolfe, and H. B. Otterman for the State Department.

151. Memorandum of 7 July meeting at State Department, "Elimination of Clandestine Radio Stations in this Hemisphere"; and memorandum from OP-20-WP-2 to OP-20-A, "Project of Detecting and Locating Clandestine Radio Transmitters in South America" (14 October 1942).

152. Memorandum from Sterling to Jett (18 July 1942).

153. Memorandum of the 14 July meeting at State Department; memorandum from Sterling to Jett (18 July 1942); letter from Long to Fly (31 July 1942); and letter from Fly to Long (8 August 1942).

154. Memorandum from Norman to Jett, "South American Radio Intelligence Program as Sponsored by the State Department of the United States of America"(21 August 1942); and memoranda from OP-20-GX to Op-20-G. "Trucks in Colombia and Ecuador (17 July 1942), and "Trucks and Associated Equipment Other Than DT Direction Finders at Colombia and Ecuador," undated. (possibly 17 July 1942). The presence at the 20 August meeting of E. P. Coffee and R. E. Thornton of the FBI marked the FBI's first participation in the program. Tbe FBI representatives seemed interested only as the program related to FBI radio activities in Latin America.

155. Memorandum from Sterling to Jett (14 October 1942); and a memorandum from Sterling to Jett (15 October 1942), "Supplemental Memorandum (Off-the-Record Comment) Concerning the South American Project."

156. Letters to R. D. Linx: and J. F. de Bardeleban from S. W. Norman (7 March 1942); letter from Chairman Fly to A. A. Berle (13 March 1942); memorandum from LCDR Welker to OP-20-G (19 March 1942); Sterling memorandum of 10 October 1942 and letters to the selectees on the same date; Sterling letters to F. C. de Wolfe on 28 October and 2 November 1942; letters from Chairman Fly to Secretary Welles, 28 March and 6 April 1942; letter from Ambassador Braden to the Secretary of State (11 July 1942); and a report of a meeting of 20 March 1942. The 20 March meeting was attended by ADM Hooper, LCDR Alwin D. Kramer. LCDR G. W. Welker, and LCDR F. C. B. Jordan for the Navy; MAJ S. C. Canova (USA) for the Defense Aid Division, Office of the Undersecretary of War; and for the Cubans: Colonel Antonio Bolet, Chief of the Engineering Corps, Cuban Army; Lieutenant Colonel Felipe Morilla, the Cuban Military Attaché; and Lieutenant Felipe Gadenas, the Cuban Naval Attaché.

157. Memorandum from MAJ Harry I. Marks, Acting Chief, Communications Branch, AIC. to George Sterling (17 November 1942); Sterling memorandum to MAJ Marks (4 December 1942); letter from Fly to Assistant Secretary of State Long, 4 December, and Long's answer of 6 December 1942; COL Collins' letter to CPT William Barclay Harding, Chief, Operations and Contact Section, AIS, undated; State Department order of 16 December to U.S. diplomatic officers in Latin America; letter orders to the selectees sent on 26 December 1942; and a memorandum of the 7 January 1943 meeting.

158. "Agreement between FBI and MID for the Operation of a Network to Locate Clandestine Radio Stations in Latin America, and tbe Action to Be Taken upon the Information Derived Therefrom" (1 December 1942). This agreement was signed by RADM H. C. Train, DNI; J. Edgar Hoover, Director of the FBI; and MG George V. Strong, Assistant Chief of Staff, G-2.

159. Memorandum from S. W. Norman (10 August 1942); and letters from Norman to Breckenridge Long on 18 August and from Ambassador Braden to the Secretary of State on 8 September 1942.

160. Letter from Ambassador Braden to the Secretary of State, "Radio Transmission and Radio Monitoring in Cuba" (17 October 1942); and "Special Report on Caba,"

a report from Charles B. Hogg to the Chief, RID, dated 26 October 1943.

161. Report from de Bardeleban, "Review of Chilean Assignment, March 1942-March 1943" (20 April 1943).

162. Letters from Sterling to Fellows (31 October and 11 December 1942); cable from G. H. Goeman to the Chief, RID (20 March 1943): letter from Chairman Fly to the Secretary of State (26 March 1943); cable from de Bardeleben to Sterling (31 March 19431 and amplifying letter of the same date: and memorandum from Sterling to de Bardeleban, "Duty Assignment" (5 April 1943).

163. Memorandum from McDermott to Sterling, "WACA B7," undated; and letter from de Bardeleban to Sterling giving a final report on the Argentinian operation, dated 12 March 1944. "WACA B7" was the FCC case notation for the Argentinian clandestine net.

164. Memorandum from the Chief, U.S. Naval Mission to Ecuador, to Vice Chief of Naval Operations, "Radio Direction Finder Unit — Report of Activities for the Month of January 1943" (31 January 1943).

165. Letters from Charles R. Week. to the Chief, AIS (11 May 1943): and to George Sterling (16 February 1943); and memoranda from the Vice Chief of Naval Operations to the Chief, U.S. Naval Mission to Ecuador, "Transfer of Radio Direction Finder Equipment Presently Located in Ecuador to the War Department" (5 January 1943); from OP-20-G to OP-20, "Navy High-Frequency Direction Finder Equipment Loaned to Ecuador and Colombia, Facts Concerning" (9 January 1943); cable from BUPERS to ALUSNA Quito (9 March 19431), cable from Vice Chief of Naval Operations to ALUSNA Quito (24 March 1943); and memorandum from U.S. Naval Attaché, Quito, to the Vice Chief of Naval Operations, "Radio Direction Finder Equipment, Transfer to U.S. Military Attaché, Quito, Ecuador" (27 March 1943).

166. U.S. Military Attaché Report 1842, "Radio Intelligence Service of Colombian Ministry of War" (18 November 1942); and memorandum from VCNO to Chief, U.S. Naval Mission to Ecuador (11 January 1943).

167. Memoranda from Strong to the Chief, RID, "Report of Progress in Bogotá, Colombia" (26 January 1943 and 6 April 1943); letter from the Chairman, FCC, to Assistant Secretary of State C. Howland Shaw (14 April 1943); Strong's report to the Chief, RID (26 April 1943); memorandum from Sterling to Jett concerning

extension of TDYs (14 May 1943); and letter from Strong to COL Marks, AIS (13 June 1943).

168. Memorandum from Norman to Linx (7 March 1942); letter from Fly to A. A. Berle (13 March 1942); cable from Linx to the Secretary of State (10 April 1942); Hilton's *Hitlers Secret War in South America, 1939-1946*, 240, 283; Linx's "Activity Report #8" (10 May 1942) and "Activity Report #10" (27 May 1942); and memorandum from Sterling to Jett (18 July 1942).

169. Linx's Progress Reports #15 (8 July 1942) and #16 (12 July 1942).

170. Letter from Ambassador Caffrey to the Secretary of State (27 July 1942).

171. "Report of Activities, Robert D. Linx: Week Ending September 19, 1942" (20 September 1942).

172. Memorandum from Norman to Jett, "South American Radio Intelligence Program as Sponsored by the State Department of the United States of America" (21 August 1942); Linx's Activity Report of 20 September 1942; memorandum from Sterling, to Jett concerning TDY extensions (14 May 1943); and a cable from A. A. Berle to the Secretary of State concerning Linx's return to the U.S., (28 November 1945).

173. Letter from Fly to Shaw (14 April 1943); memorandum from Sterling to Jett concerning TDY extensions (14 May 1943);memorandum from Sterling to Jett re State Department commendation of de Bardeleben (22 December 1942); letter of commendation for Robert D. Linx (3 August 1945); commendation for John Crewe from U. S. Military Attaché, Dominican Republic (21 April 1943); letter of commendation from Fly to Strong (11 October 1943); and letters of commendation from Sterling to Fellows (8 October 1943), and from Jett to Fellows (11 October 1943).

174. De Bardeleben's final report to Sterling on his tour in Argentina (12 March 1944).

175. McDermott's final report to Sterling, (undated, but probably March 1944).

176. Memorandum from BG Frank E. Stoner, Chief Army Communications Service, and COL W. Preston Corderman, Chief, Signal Security Branch, to OIC, Naval Communications Annex:, "Transfer of Certain Intercept Installations" (24 August 19441.

177. TAB B to memorandum from BG Frank E. Stoner to COL W. Preston Corderman (24 August 1944).

178. Memorandum from U.S. Naval Attaché, Bogotá, to CNO, "Transfer of Clandestine Monitoring and D/F Station to Cognizance of U.S. Naval Attaché in Bogotá" (27 December 1944).

179. Letter from ADM Ralph Bard to Secretary of State (28 February 19415).

180. Letter from Secretary of the Navy to the Secretary of State (18January 1946).

NOTES ON SOURCES

Primary Sources

Although the author cites specific documents in his notes, his citations are incomplete in that they do not include the location of the documents within the T54 holdings. His operational duties and the enormity of the task prevent him rectifying the omission. It may be stated that all of the primary sources cited are contained in the NSA Historical Collection (Series IV), and in the records of the FBI, FCC, State Department, Coast Guard, and Navy. Additional files consulted in the Historical Collection include the TICOM records, the German clandestine files, and the Roosevelt file. Readers who wish to pursue a reference should contact the NSA Historian for assistance.

Secondary Sources

Farago, Ladislas, *The Game of Foxes,* New York: David McKay, 1971.

Griffiths, LCDR L. A., *GC&CS Secret Service SIGINT, Vol. 1: Organization and Evolution of British Secret Service SIGINT.*

Hilton, Stanley E., *Hitler's Secret War in South America, 1939-1945*, Baton Rouge: Louisiana State University, 1981.

Hinsley, F. H., *British Intelligence in World War II,* Vol 1, London: HMSO, 1979.

Kahn, David, *Hitler's Spies,* New York: MacMillan, 1978.

Paine, Lauren, *German Military Intelligence in World War II: The Abwehr,* New York: Stein and Day, 1984.

Tuchman, Barbara W., *The Zimmermann Telegram,* New York: Viking Press, 1958.

PART II–THE CRYPTOLOGY OF THE GERMAN INTELLIGENCE SERVICES

Table of Contents

FOREWORD

The second part of David P. Mowry's history of German clandestine activity in South America is devoted exclusively to descriptions of the cryptographic systems used by the German intelligence organizations and their agents in South America. In fact, this detailed report covers German cryptographic systems used on a number of agent circuits in Europe as well. Mr. Mowry's interesting work invites a number of questions about German cryptography. For example, what does this collection of facts about these systems tell us about the state of German cryptography during World War II? Were these systems on a par with those of the United States, England, Japan, or more or less advanced? Were they new, obsolete, innovative, standard? Was there a correlation between the system and the level of information? And what of German security procedures and practices? Mr. Mowry has provided a valuable service in identifying and describing these systems. Perhaps future historians will attempt the challenge of answering these more general questions. It is, however, an excellent companion piece for his part one.

Henry F. Schorreck
NSA Historian
[1989]

The Cryptology of the German Intelligence Services

Introduction

Historical records concerning the exploitation of Axis clandestine traffic in World War II are few. The following account depends primarily on *GC&CS Secret Service SIGINT,* Volumes I-III, which covers 1928 to 1945; "History of OP-20-GU (Coast Guard Unit of the Naval Communications Annex)," which covers only 1941 to 30 June 1943 and is concerned primarily with administrative matters rather than the cryptanalytic effort itself; and *History of Coast Guard Unit #387, 1940-1945.* Both the Coast Guard and the British Government Code & Cipher School (GC&CS) cryptanalytic histories cover the entire war, but consist of series of technical reports on the cryptanalytic methods used, with little regard for historical continuity, and little or no traffic analytic information. In addition, there is a file of over 10,000 Coast Guard translations of clandestine messages. Because the following is a synthesis of all of the above sources, footnotes have been omitted except for information derived from Colonel Alferd McCormack's London trip report and for the descriptions of the cryptographic machines developed by Fritz Menzer of the Abwehr, which are taken from TICOM (Target Intelligence Committee) documents. This account is not to serve as a course in cryptanalysis, but rather as a description of German cryptology. The reader is referred to the appropriate histories for details of analysis.

Each of the cryptanalytic agencies at this time used its own cryptosystem titling and case notation conventions. Coast Guard system titles consisted of a letter or digraph followed by a digit. The letters were "S" for substitution systems, "T" for transposition systems, "ST" for substitution followed by transposition, and "TS" for transposition followed by substitution. The systems were numbered one-up by type. Case notations consisted of a digit, signifying geographic area, followed by one-up literal serialization within area. GC&CS broke the clandestine network down into fifteen groups, notated I to XV. Individual links or "services" received a digital notation so that, for example, Stuttgart-St. Jean de Luz was notated X/290 and Paris-Wiesbaden was notated III/20. Unfortunately, no equation list for the British notation system has been found. Cryptosystems were referred to by the link notation. In the following discussion, terminals will be given when known.

Code Systems

On 1 January 1940, messages encrypted with a dictionary code were intercepted on the Mexico-Nauen commercial circuit. Only eleven letters were used in the transmission: A, C, E, D, H, K, L, N, R, U, and W, with N having the highest frequency. It was apparent that a letter-for-number substitution was being used, with N as a separator. Anagramming the letters gave the result

D	U	R	C	H	W	A	L	K	E	N
1	2	3	4	5	6	7	8	9	0	-

Thus, the text

```
UHHNR   LNDAL   NURND   WCNCK ...
```

became

```
255-38   178-23   184-79   ...
```

Three other key words were used during the effective period of the system. All were easily recovered. All of the 1940-1941 messages in this system were sent with the addresses SUDAMERIAT. WEDEKIND, SUDAMERO, or EGMARSUND.

Similar traffic was sent from Chile to BACOCHASE in March 1942, signed by the German ambassador to Chile. In these messages ten-letter key words were used with the other sixteen letters of the alphabet serving as separators. Eventually it was determined that the dictionary used was Langenscheidt's *Spanish-German Pocket Dictionary*. With this discovery all messages were completely decrypted.

With the beginning of the war in Europe, the Coast Guard was tasked with the collection of commercial circuits between the Western Hemisphere and Germany. This collection revealed that many Axis-dominated commercial firms in Mexico and Central and South America were using enciphered commercial codes in their communications with Germany.

The largest group of messages in enciphered commercial code used the Rudolph Mosse code with the letters of each code group transposed and a monoalphabetic substitution applied to the last two letters of the transposed group. These messages used the indicator OPALU as the first group of text (A1 group). Traffic was passed to and from SUDAMERO and SUDAMERIAT, Mexico; SUDAMERIAT, Hamburg; and SUDAMVORST, SUDAMERO, and SUDAMERIAT, Berlin.

In August 1941 traffic from SOLINGEN in Nauen, Germany, to BOKER in Mexico used the same code book with a subtracter of seven applied to each letter (i.e., EMUAS became XANTL). Other variations were noted: in 1941, MUENCHIMPO, Hamburg, used a mixed arrangement of Rudolph Mosse and Peterson codes and other links used Acme, Peterson, Mosse or Alpha codes either enciphered or in combination with one another.

Three other codes were intercepted, with two of them designed for encoding stereotyped weather messages. The Dago code (GC&CS terminology), used by German ships in the Baltic Sea, encrypted figures with a daily-changing key and encoded words with a two-letter code. A sliding code was used by all of the German trawlers in the Ijmuiden. Two sliding strips were used with clear values on a fixed table, with single-letter code values on one strip and mononome or dinome code values on the other. The A1 group of each message gave the position of each strip against an index mark and the number of characters in the message. Circuit II/405's five-letter code used the International Signalbuch with a simple substitution applied to the first character of each group.

Monoalphabetic Substitution

Only four monoalphabetic substitution systems were used by the German agent organization. The first of these was initially intercepted on the England-Germany circuit in October 1940. The preamble consisted of two four-letter and two three-letter groups which contained the date and time of encryption, character count, and serial number, encrypted with a monoalphabetic letter-for-figure substitution. The alphabets used in encrypting both the preambles and the messages were derived from a disk. There were two parts to the disk, each of which carried an alphabet and a series of numbers and could be rotated relative to the other. Each agent was assigned a fixed key letter. This letter, on the inner disk, would be set against the date (mod 26) on the outer disk. Plain values on the inner disk were then encrypted with cipher values from the outer disk. The numbers in both the preamble and in the text were similarly encrypted. OP-20-G interpreted the observed phenomena as a Vigenére Square with progress through the square governed by the date, with a separate key used to encipher numbers in the text. The underlying plain text was English. The British were notified and it was later learned that they had arrested the agent and taken over his station. (Author's note: This was possibly the agent SNOW mentioned in part one.)

Circuit X/203, a ship, used a letter-for-figure substitution for encrypting its weather reports which consisted entirely of figures. Twelve different keys were used. The preamble consisted of the Q-signal QTT followed by a three-letter group. The first and third letters of this group were the equivalents of one and two, respectively, in the key being used.

A third system, referred to by the British as the Wigo cipher, was a dinomic substitution without variants sent in five-figure groups. The $Z1$ group of the message gave a character count and the $Z0$ identified the substitution set. The users of this system were never identified.

The only other monoalphabetic substitution system noted, first intercepted on the Hamburg-Cape Spartel circuit in January 1945, was used to report convoys spotted off Cape Spartel. The plain text was Spanish, and eight substitution systems were used in daily rotation.

Polyalphabetic Substitution

A number of links used variations on Gronsfeld polyalpbabetic substitution, where all cipher alphabets were direct standard with the offset from the plain component determined by a running key. The maximum offset, therefore, was nine.

The "French Gronsfelds" used on II/320 and II/321 used a fixed 20-long key; while II/335 used daily-changing, variable-length keys. No indicators were used.

One variation on Gronsfeld cipher was used by an agent in England to communicate with his headquarters in occupied France. The system, referred to by the British as the Constantinople cipher, used the word "Constantinople" to derive the daily key. A numerical key was derived in the normal way and then multiplied by the date. Thus, for the eighth of the month

```
CONS T ANT INO P LE
2961213171448101153
                 x8
2368970637158480 9224
```

In October 1941, Rio de Janeiro was intercepted using a seven-alphabet Gronsfeld with a key of 3141592. Since 3141592 is the decimal equivalent of the mathematical constant *pi*, this circuit was dubbed "the *pi* circuit."

The so-called "Dutch Gronsfelds" were not, strictly speaking, true Gronsfelds, since the slide of one alphabet against the other could exceed nine letters. The term is somewhat justified, however, by the fact that the different shifts of the slide used in encrypting a message never differed by more than nine. The key was periodic, based on the date, with two digits always used for the day and one or two digits for the month. Thus, 2 March was represented by 023 and 25 December by 2512. These figures were converted to letters by a daily-changing key to give a three- or four-letter key. In encipherment, the first letter of the key in the cipher component was aligned with *A* on the plain component and the first letter of text was enciphered; the second letter of the key was aligned with *A* and the second letter was enciphered, and so on, repeating the key as often as necessary.

All of the above used direct standard alphabets. Some other circuits used random mixed alphabets. The "Spanish Substitutions" used tables of five random cipher alphabets in various ways, while the "Bordeaux Substitutions" used tables of five or ten alphabets. The BF cipher used a 21-long key to encrypt traffic passed on the Nantes-Paris-St.-Jean-de-Luz circuit. Keys were changed infrequently, and the traffic could be identified by the letters "BF" in the preamble. The X/203 circuit, mentioned above, used a ten-alphabet substitution for traffic other than weather. The starting alphabet was indicated by a number in the preamble. That alphabet was then used to encipher the first five letters; the next alphabet enciphered the next five letters, etc., cycling after the tenth alphabet.

Much later, in 1944-1945, the Shanghai-Canton circuit used a periodic polyalphabetic system to pass information concerning air traffic between China and India, United States aid to China, United

States planes and equipment, and information and rumors concerning Russia. Each message used five alphabets taken from a twenty-four-alphabet Latin square. The alphabets to be used in each case were indicated by a five-letter A1/Z0 indicator. Each alphabet served as both plain and cipher component, offset according to a key derived from the date of the message.

Digraphic Substitution

Two digraphic substitution systems were used. The first, a double-square Playfair system was used according to normal rules. The second used a Playfair-like square in which any character from the same column as the plain letter could be used as a column coordinate and any character from the same row as the plain letter could be used as a row coordinate. Thus, in the square

```
N A T I O
L S E C U
R Y G B D
F H K M P
O V W X Z
```

the letter P could be represented by sixteen different digraphs:

OF UF DF ZF OH UH DH ZH
OK UK DK ZK OM UM DM ZM

As used on the Cologne-Maastricht circuit, the letter *J* was omitted from the square. The key was changed monthly, but only one key was broken since the traffic had no particular value. On another circuit, the underlying plain was in French and the letter *K* was omitted. In this case, ten nontextual letters at the beginning of text probably constituted a concealed preamble enciphered with a key.

Single Transposition: Columnar

The story of the VVV TEST-AOR circuit has already been told in part one. In January 1941, when the FBI asked the Coast Guard for assistance in the solution of a group of messages, examination revealed that they were copies of the traffic being relayed from GLENN to AOR through VVV TEST. The system was diagnosed as a simple columnar transposition and solved. Traffic on the VVV TEST-AOR circuit used a 20-wide key. The relay traffic turned out to be in two systems: a simple columnar transposition using a 16-wide key that was later reversed and then replaced by a 23-wide key; and a grille transposition which will be described later.

In April 1941 Coast Guard intercept operators found another circuit with the same characteristics as the VVV TEST-AOR circuit, using the callsigns HEW and PYL. The control sounded very much like AOR. The A1-A4 groups of the messages, enciphered by a number key, contained date, time, and character count. Traffic on this circuit read as columnar transposition on a 20-wide key. This key was later reversed and still later replaced by another 20-wide key. In June 1941 Hamburg instructed the outstation Valparaiso to use the Albatross edition of the novel *South Latitude* as a key book. In the use of this key book, the agent was assigned a secret number which, when added to the date and the number of the month, designated the page from which the number key and transposition key were to be extracted. Dummy letters were inserted in the plain text according to the transposition key for the first 100 letters of text. For example, if the key began 18, 20, 15, 11, ..., the first dummy character was inserted in the 18th position, the second twenty letters after that, the third fifteen letters after that, etc. In the second 100 letters, the dummies were placed so as to reflect those in the first 100, making a symmetrical pattern.

The Belgium-France-England circuits were similar to the above, except that the keys varied in length from circuit to circuit, keys were taken from a line of a key page, there were no dummies, and the key page was given by an indicator inserted in a fixed position in the message.

Two Hamburg-Rio de Janeiro circuits were sister circuits that came up at approximately the same time. The key books for these circuits were the Albatross editions of *In the Midst of Life and The Story of Bon Michele*. On one of these circuits, the agent's secret number was added to the date plus eight times the number of the month to determine the page from which the key was to be extracted. Traffic on the Bremen-Rio de Janeiro circuit had "buried" indicator groups at A4 and A6. Breaking these out with a key number gave the date, time, two-figure serial number, and two-figure key number.

given in A-7abc and the dummy pattern identified in the A-7de.

In the system used by Stettin-controlled stations, one basic key word provided all the keys. Key 01 was derived in the normal manner. For subsequent keys the key word was permuted cyclically (see figure 1). Key lengths varied considerably from circuit to circuit. Dummies were placed according to the transposition key as on Hamburg-controlled circuits. The preamble gave the key number and the character count.

Key Word:	A	N	T	E	N	N	E	N	A	N	L	A	G	E	A	N	T	E	N
Key 01	1	9	14	4	10	11	5	12	2	13	8	3	7	6					
Key 02		9	14	4	10	11	5	12	1	13	8	2	7	6	3				
Key 03			14	4	9	10	5	11	1	12	8	2	7	6	3	13			
Key 04				4	9	10	5	11	1	12	8	2	7	6	3	13	14		
Key 05					9	10	4	11	1	12	8	2	7	5	3	13	14	6	
Key 06						9	4	10	1	11	8	2	7	5	3	12	14	6	13

Fig. 1. Derivation of Stettin transposition keys

On the Lisbon-Portuguese Guinea circuit, the A10 group contained the key indicator enciphered with the key number. Text was inscribed boustrophedonically in columns with dummies at the top of columns 1 and 11, in the second position in groups 2 and 12, in the third position in 3 and 13, etc. Long messages were broken into 10-deep matrices, each separately transposed. On Lisbon-Lourenco Marques the A8bcd (the middle three letters of the A8 group) constituted the page indicator to an unknown book. All columns read downward, with dummies at the top of columns 1 and 9, in second place in 2 and 10, etc. Messages were transposed in toto, not broken up into multiple matrices. On the Lisbon-North America circuit, the indicator was in the A5bcd. Key length was 17 and dummies were placed at the top of columns 1 and 10, in second position in 2 and 11, etc. The dummy pattern was reflected after nine lines. Messages from America began with an internal serial number. The messages on the Lisbon-Azores circuit carried a character count in the preamble with the key page

On the Stuttgart-Libya circuit the key word appeared in the cipher text inserted one letter at a time in prearranged positions, namely,

01	07	13	19	25
26	32	38	44	50
51	57	63	..	..

The preamble gave a character count, the middle or first digit of which gave the position of an indicator group. For the purpose of writing in the key word, this indicator group counted as a textual group, and one of its letters was a letter of the key word. The other four letters gave the length of the key word enciphered twice, each on a different key number.

Single Transposition: Combs and Grilles

The comb transposition system used on Cologne-Rio de Janeiro used the "Bluejacket" edition of the King James Version of the Bible as a key source. This circuit used daily changing callsigns, and the specific indicator for the date of encryption was given by including the callsign for that date in the preamble. This date determined the page of the key book from which the key was extracted.

Page = 30 x number of month x date x 10

The number "10" above was a secret agent number assigned to this agent for the year 1941. It was changed to "20" in 1942. This gave a page range of 41-401 for 1941 and 51-411 for 1942.

Figure 2 illustrates the encryption process using Genesis 1:1 as key. Inscribed across the top of the matrix, the key phrase determined the order of

transposition of columns. Odd-numbered columns were extracted from top to bottom, even-numbered columns from bottom to top. Written down the left side of the matrix, the position of each letter of the key phrase in the standard alphabet determined the length of that line in the matrix.

In the case of Hamburg-Sao Paulo, only the Hamburg terminal was ever heard, and only five messages were read. After the agent involved was arrested in 1943, it was discovered that the initial key had been INCONSTITUTIONALISAMENTE. After contact was established, keys were taken from the book *Pagel in Glueck.* When the agent was apprehended, he turned over a copy of *The Martyrdom of Man,* which was to have replaced *Pagel in Glueck.* The key page was determined by adding the agent number to the day of the year.

```
NALHN   UCNED   LMNOH   NLDLE   EKHNP   NMLND
EEAUL   LEOWE   RSDED   SKFRS   FXONU   SMVCS
REEMT   THTNA   EIINE   ECXOS   USCCO   XPAFU
EHUUT   HTLLT   XNDEH   OSTOI   EDNDA   NUMNO
ILATT   EDIMU   TMINM   HIEIF   MEIHT   ..... etc.
```

Fig. 2b. Test after comb transposition

Only six keys were recovered on Hamburg-Lisbon, and the key book, which was in either Spanish or Portuguese, was never determined.

Grilles were sheets of cardboard divided into squares with some of the squares cut out. Plain text was written into the cutout squares horizontally and extracted vertically by key. Dummy characters were inserted in prearranged squares (see fig. 3a). The grille could be used directly or in reverse (i.e., turned over) and in any one of four orientations, giving eight possible positions for anyone grille.

Late in the autumn of 1940, intercept operators collecting the Chapultepec-Nauen ILC circuit intercepted some suspicious traffic from cable address VOLCO in Mexico City to BRAJOB in Berlin. These cable addresses were later changed to GESIK and INTERCIALE. In contrast to the commercial code

```
          I N T H E B E G I N N I N G G O D C R E
          1 1 2 1           1 1 1 1 1       1       1
          1 4 0 0 4 1 6 7 2 6 8 3 7 8 9 8 3 2 9 6

I   9 D E I N E N R V I
N  14 E R X X W A S C H B E R I C
T  20 H T E T O L D S M O B I L E X O L D S M
H   8 O B I L E M E R
E   6 S T E L L
B   2 T M
E   6 O N A T L
G   7 I C H H U N D
I   9 E R T T A U S E N
N  14 D S T U E C K E I N S F U E
N  14 N F F U E N F M M X M M U N
I   9 D H U N D E R T T
N  14 A U S E N D S T U E C K E I
G   7 N S N U L L F
G   7 U E N F M M X
O  15 M M C A N N O N M U N I T I O
D   4 N X X P
C   3 O N T
R  18 I A C X P O N T I A C H E R S T E L
E   6 L T M O N
A   1 A
T  20 T L I C H H U N D E R T T A U S E N D S
E   6 T U E C K
D   4 E I N S
```

Fig. 2a. Comb transposition matrix

traffic usually intercepted on ILC, this traffic was evidently transposed German text using low frequency letters as nulls. Further analysis determined that an overlay of some sort, with two sides was being used. This overlay had 135 open cells (twenty-seven five-letter groups) with certain cells marked for the insertion of nulls. In figure 3, lowercase letters are nulls; the plain text is the same as in figure 2. Any one of the eight corners of the grille (obverse or reverse) could be placed in the upper left-hand corner.

		1				1					1	1
4	8	2	5	1	6	3	7	9	3	2	0	1
D	•	E	I	N	E	•	N	R	V	•	I	E
•	R	X	•	•	X	W	A	S	•	C	•	H
•	B	v	•	E	•	•	•	p	R	•	I	•
C	H	•	T	•	E	T	O	L	•	•	•	D
•	•	S	•	M	•	•	•	O	B	•	I	L
E	X	•	O	•	L	D	•	•	S	M	O	•
•	•	B	I	L	•	E	•	m	•	•	H	•
E	k	•	•	•	R	S	T	•	E	L	•	•
•	•	L	T	j	M	•	•	O	•	•	N	A
T	L	•	•	I	C	H	•	•	H	U	•	•
•	•	N	D	•	•	E	•	R	T	•	T	•
A	U	•	•	S	E	N	•	D	S	T	•	U
•	•	E	•	•	•	g	C	•	•	K	E	•
•	I	N	f	•	S	•	•	F	U	•	E	N
F	•	•	F	•	•	U	•	•	E	N	F	•
•	c	•	•	M	•	•	M	•	•	b	•	•
•	•	M	M	•	U	N	•	D	•	H	U	•
N	D	•	E	•	R	•	T	T	A	•	U	S
•	•	E	•	N	D	S	•	T	•	U	E	•

Fig. 3a. Grille Transposition Matrix (Lower case letters are dummies.)

Although the system is technically only a single transposition, the method effectively prevented solution by the normal method of matching columns and anagramming the resulting rows. Since there were no stereotyped beginnings or endings in this traffic, the solution of single messages of fewer than fifty-four groups presented a problem so difficult that not all of the messages in this system were ever read.

```
NEMLJ ISMNU HBNKT ULMCV RBSEH
TSUEA NFATE ECDIT OITDF FMEDR
USECM RLEXE NAOTC MTDCI ULKXH
BRRSP LOMOR DFDTT EUUFE ETNHO
IIIEH DLAUN XSEMN ENLBS VXEWT
DESHE NGUNS
```

Fig. 3b. Sample of grille-transposed text

Some traffic in this system was also sent from GLENN to AOR via VVV TEST. The system was also discovered being used in secret ink messages carried out of Mexico by couriers. These were labeled the *Max Code* by the Germans.

In September 1941 Berlin-Rio de Janeiro stopped using simple transposition. The system introduced used the same type of indicator as that used on the BRAJOB-VOLCO circuit: the A3abc identified a key page and the A3d identified the upper left corner of the grille. The grille used proved to be the same as the BRAJOB-VOLCO grille with 125 open cells instead of 135.

Traffic intercepted on the Madrid-West Africa circuit also used the 13 X 19 grille, but with 1S6 open cells; the same size grille as used by Paris had 140 open cells. The Las Palmas-Cisneros grille was only 9 x 13 with 88 open cells, while the grille used on the Bulogne-Ostend-Brussels-Lille circuit was 15 x 21 with 224 open cells.

It is interesting to note the degree of security which the German authorities believed this system possessed. After the rupture in German-Brazilian relations and during the German spy roundup in Brazil, German Foreign Office dispatches were sent over the Madrid-West Africa circuit in this system, when commercial circuits could no longer be used.

Aperiodic Polyalphabetic Substitution

These systems were encountered after the roundup of German spies in Brazil. Immediately after the Brazilian arrests, two new circuits were found which had the transmission characteristics of Hamburg-controlled agent communications: daily changing callsigns, slow transmission speed, and voluminous "ham" chatter. The cipher system used was "running key," i.e., one in which the juxtaposition of two sliding alphabets is determined by a continuous aperiodic key, usually taken from a book or magazine. It was known that the Germans preferred to equip their agents with systems in which the elements could be memorized and used in combination with a popular novel or other innocent book; and it was hoped that either direct or reverse standard alphabets had been employed for the plain and cipher components. Such proved to be the case and decryption of messages revealed that the new circuit was a Hamburg-Chile one, which while it did not replace the previous Hamburg-Chile circuit, reported the same type of information. Intercepted traffic contained information on U.S. equipment and ship movements. It was later learned that the Spanish book *Sonar la Vida* was used for the key source. The A1-A4 groups contained an enciphered preamble, and the AS group usually contained the same letter repeated three times. After the system had been analyzed and some messages read, it was determined that the repeated letter was the reference letter used for sliding the plain and cipher components.

The other circuit which appeared in March 1942 linked Hamburg and Lisbon and passed information concerning the movement of Allied vessels to and from Lisbon. The key book in this case was eventually identified as the Portuguese novel *O Servo de Deus*. This circuit departed from normal agent communications procedures in that it used multiple frequencies on multiple schedules. The Lisbon terminal was assigned as many as eight different frequencies. Later these were changed weekly for greater security.

Another user never became fully operative. For several months Hamburg repeatedly sent what appeared to be seven different encipherments of the same two messages. No contact was ever made and transmissions usually ceased. In this case the plain text was in German with a Portuguese running key.

A new circuit out of Rio de Janeiro began operation in June 1942 using a running-key system. Traffic was very irregular and was concerned primarily with administrative matters. Both key and plain text were in German, but the book was never identified.

On the Stuttgart-St.-Jean-de-Luz circuit the preamble gave the character count and the penultimate digit of this number gave the position of the indicator. The indicator was five-letter, with the "ab" positions giving the page and the "cd" positions the line, both enciphered with a letter-for-figure number key. The "e" position identified the index letter to be used. Messages with ER in the preamble used a German key book to encipher German text. Other messages used a Spanish key book to encipher Spanish and occasionally German text.

A running-key system used in France was sent with the indicator in the A1 group in January and July, in the A2 group in February and August, etc., and in the Z0 group. On some links the key was in French. The fixed index letter was "Z."

Single Transposition/Substitution Systems

Around the end of 1942, the Hamburg-Bordeaux circuit used a 16-wide simple columnar transposition in conjunction with a trivial monoalphabetic substitution. Long after the fact, it was learned that this circuit had used the "Janowski" (see below) system with a 16-wide key from July to November 1942. It had then changed over to the transposition/substitution system, which remained in effect until April 1943 when the Janowski encipherment was reintroduced, this time with a 22-wide key.

In the latter part of February 1943, the FCC provided the Coast Guard with intercept of an unknown circuit controlled by Hamburg. The traffic, intercepted in November and December t942, included three messages of eleven groups each which matched two eleven group messages intercepted by the Coast Guard on the same circuit in January and February 1943. The Coast Guard had already determined that a simple substitution using standard alphabets was involved with the resulting intermediate plain text transposed. Analysis of the five equal-length messages revealed the existence of a comb transposition matrix with a 21-long key which was finally determined to be *Ueb immer Treu und Redlichkeit* ("always practice loyalty and integrity"). The A1 group was the indicator for the substitution. Two standard alphabets were juxtaposed so that the A1b was the cipher equivalent of the A1a. The outstation on this circuit never responded by radio, but was apparently in South America.

The system referred to by the British as the "Bloodhound Cipher" was used on the Bremen-Bayonne circuit. It was a single transposition system substituted in columns.

The 26-long transposition key was made up of twenty-five consecutive letters from a lengthy key phrase. The starting point was determined by adding the date and the month.

Substitution was performed after the plain text had been written into the transposition matrix, and was based on a fixed substitution key,

```
             1 1 1 1 1 1 1 1 1 1 2 2 2 2 2 2
1 2 3 4 5 6 7 8 9 0 1 2 3 4 5 6 7 8 9 0 1 2 3 4 5
G M V W L B C U T S D I Q Y X E O J F K A P R N H
```

that is, "G" was the key for column 1, "M" for column 2, etc.

The message key letter to be used was determined by subtracting 2 from the date; thus, on the sixth of the month the key letter would be "D," the

fourth letter of the alphabet. Two direct standard alphabets were used for encipherment with the message key letter set against the appropriate letter of the substitution key. In this case, "D" plain would be set against "G" cipher for column 1. Substitution for the 1st, 4th, 7th, 10th, etc. letters of the column was normal. For enciphering the 2nd, 5th, 8th, etc. letters, the plain component was moved one space to the right of the initial setting; and for the 3rd, 6th, 9th, etc., and the plain component was moved one space to the left of the initial setting. For instance, if the first column read

```
E
N
X
B
W
N
```

setting "D" plain to "o" cipher would give

```
Plain:  X Y Z A B C D E F G H I J K L M N O P Q R S T U V W
Cipher: A B C D E F G H I J K L M N O P Q R S T U V W X Y Z
```

and the column would be enciphered

```
E = H
N = R
X = Z
B = E
W = A
N = P
```

After the substitution was performed, columns were extracted from the bottom upward. The indicator was in the A3 group with the A3ad being the first two letters of the transposition key.

In December 1942 the Royal Canadian Mounted Police provided the Coast Guard with the record of a German agent named Janowski, who had been arrested in Canada in November. Among the materials turned over were two novels which were to be used to generate his encryption keys. The agent's number, 28 in this case, added to the number of the month and date, gave the page of the book to be used. Messages had a five-group preamble enciphered with two keys: one for the first four groups which contained transmission date, time, character count, and serial number, and the second for the fifth group which contained the date of encryption. In this system, the Janowski method (see fig. 4), the text was first written horizontally into a transposition rectangle and extracted according to a 20-long key derived from the first twenty letters reading downward from the top left-hand corner of the page for the day (see fig. 4a). Substitution was performed on each column separately by means of a substitu-

```
    W R V C S L P T H F A S F P A A G M A Q
    2 1 1   1 1 1 1     1   1       1   1
    0 5 9 5 6 0 2 8 9 8 1 7 7 3 2 3 8 1 4 4
```

Fig. 4a. Janowski transposition key

```
    2 1 1   1 1 1 1     1   1       1   1
    0 5 9 5 6 0 2 8 9 8 1 7 7 3 2 3 8 1 4 4
    D E I N E N R V I E R X X W A S C H B E
    R I C H T E T O L D S M O B I L E X O L
    D S M O B I L E H E R S T E L L T M O N
    A T L I C H H U N D E R T T A U S E N D
```

Fig. 4b. Transposition rectangle

tion key derived from the first twenty letters reading downward from the top left-hand comer of the page for the first of the month. The substitution key was slid against a stationary standard alphabet using as an index the letter in the top left-hand corner of the day page. Substitution was column by column with the key number corresponding to the column number set against the index. In figure

```
    T W B T M K G K M A T H T M Q T B Q T B
    1 2   1         1   1   1 1 1 1     1 1
    4 0 2 5 9 7 5 8 0 1 6 6 7 1 2 8 3 3 9 4
```

Fig. 4c. Substitution Key

4c, the strips are set up for enciphering column 1. Figure 4d shows a sample substitution.

Fig. 4d. Substitution

Subsequently, seven circuits were noted using Janowski method with, at most, minor variations in indicator placement and encipherment procedure: Hamburg-Spain, Hamburg-Gijon (Spain), Hamburg-Madrid, Hamburg-Lisbon, Hamburg-Vigo (Spain), Hamburg-Bordeaux, and Hamburg-Tangier.

On the Hamburg-Spain circuit, Hamburg started by sending two messages. Two days later another two messages were sent. When compared, it was obvious that the second transmission was a repeat of the first with a different encipherment. Further examination revealed that both messages of the first transmission tested for substitution, as did the second message of the second transmission. The first message of the second transmission tested for transposition. When the two first messages were superimposed, it was found that each segment of the transposed version equated to a segment of the substituted version. This stripped off the substitution, determined the number of columns, and fixed the column lengths, all in one operation. All that remained was the anagramming of one message, and two keys were recovered simultaneously. This constituted one of the worst breaches of communications security encountered by the Coast Guard. Unfortunately, no further traffic was passed on this circuit.

Only two variations were noted in the use of Janowski. Hamburg-Gijon used a constant key for a short time before shifting to book key, and

Hamburg-Bordeaux used a 16-long key from July to November 1942, at which time the circuit changed over to the transposition substitution system previously described. In April and May 1943, Hamburg-Bordeaux again used Janowski, this time with a 22-wide key.

Two versions of substitution with grille transposition were used. The simpler method used three simple substitution tables for the 1st to the 10th of the month, the 11th to the 20th, and the 21st to the 31st. Normal grilles were used, but the spaces for dummy letters were filled with plain text. On the Madrid-San Sebastian circuit, a five-alphabet periodic substitution was applied to the plain text which was then written into the grille and extracted by key. Later, the plain text was written into the grille and extracted by key, after which the substitution was performed. Some of the links that used this system used dummies, others did not. Indicators were the same as for normal grille usage; each circuit had only one substitution table.

Double Transposition

The four circuits using double transposition, all in late 1942, were Berlin-Madrid, Berlin-Tetuan (Morocco), Berlin-Teheran, and Berlin-Argentina.

The first system of this type the Coast Guard successfully solved was intercepted on Berlin-Madrid in late 1942. Inspection revealed that the A1/A2 and Z1/Z0 groups contained a repeated enciphered indicator which deciphered as follows:

1. The first three digits ranged under 400, probably indicating the pages of a book.
2. The next two digits ranged low enough to be a line indicator.
3. The next four digits consisted of two pairs, each ranging from 10 to 30.
4. The last digit was not significant.

It seemed obvious that the two dinomes ranging from 10 to 30 were indicators designating the length of keys to be selected for a double transposi-

tion. A search was made for a message in which the length of the text equaled the product of the two keys. This constitutes a classic case for solution since such a situation nullifies the transposition. After initial success in this case, various other cases were also solved in which the message lengths bore specific relationships to the products of key widths. In November 1943 the indicator was reduced to one numerical group which the British believed designated the page number in the first three digits and the line number in the last two. A constant five-figure group was added to this indicator using non-carrying arithmetic. From the line so determined, the first four words were selected as first key, and the first four words of the next line were selected as second key. Since no solution for the additive was ever obtained, no traffic in the newer system was ever read.

In traffic on the Berlin-Tetuan circuit, the indicator initially consisted of a single group, giving only the date of encipherment. This was sufficient because there were only seven keys used for the first transposition, one for each day of the week, and the key for the second transposition was weekly changing. On 1 April 1943 the indicator was changed to one similar to the first system used on Berlin-Madrid. On 4 November 1943 the indicator was again changed, in the same fashion as Berlin-Madrid, and solutions ceased. Keys on this circuit were derived from a German translation of a British detective story.

In the Berlin-Teheran traffic, the dates were sent unenciphered in the preamble. The only other possible indicator was a number in the preamble which looked like a serial number, but which did not run in sequence. Although a few messages were solved individually, it was not until the German agent in Teheran was caught in the autumn of 1943 and the record of his interrogation forwarded to the Coast Guard that the remainder of the traffic on this circuit could be read. The complete literal key was the following six-line verse:

Wer wagt es Rittersman oder Kaapp	[Who will risk it, knight or squire
Zu taugen in diesen Schlund?	To faithfully serve in this abyss?
Einen goldenen Becher warf ich hinab	I hurl a golden chalice down,
Venrschlungen schon hat ihn der schwarse Mund	A black mouth engulfs it all around
Wer mir den Becher kann wieder zigen	But whoever makes it again be shown,
Er mag ihn behalten, er ist sein eigen	He shall retain it, for it's his own.]

The month determined the pair of lines from which the numerical key was derived; the date determined the number of the letter in this pair of lines with which the literal key started; the month then determined the minimum number of letters taken from this point for the first key; and the month finally determined the number or letters transposed from the beginning to the end of the first key to give the second key. Figure 5 shows the way in which the month controlled the key. It should be noted that if after counting the minimum number or letters, the end of a word had not been reached, the word was completed.

The Berlin-Argentina circuit was actually a number of circuits operating in and around Buenos Aires, several of them simultaneously. A variety of systems were employed on these circuits during the time they were intercepted, but double transposition was the only hand system used. The first such traffic was transmitted in November 1942, but it did not start appearing regularly until January 1943. The Coast Guard had no success with the system until GC&CS solved a 16 March 1943 message and passed the keys on to OP-2O-GU. The only apparent indicator was a preamble number similar to that found on Berlin-Teheran. The first key was a constant, of which four were used: SONDESCHLUESSEL (probe key), GASGESELLSCHAFT (gas company), SCHAEFFNER (conductor), and a fourth that apparently was the true name of the agent, NOORD. This last key was recovered, but the name could not be reconstructed. The second transposition key was a spell of the three-figure preamble group.

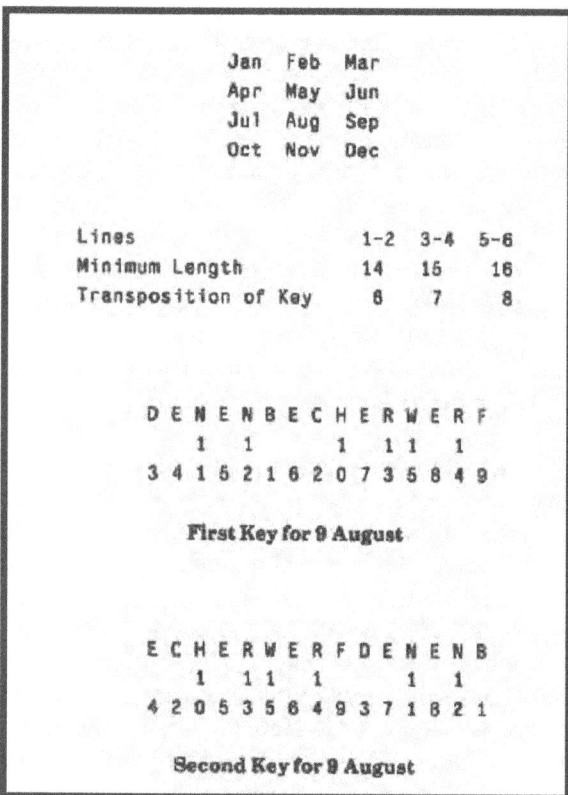

```
              Jan  Feb  Mar
              Apr  May  Jun
              Jul  Aug  Sep
              Oct  Nov  Dec


Lines                    1-2  3-4  5-6
Minimum Length            14   15   16
Transposition of Key       6    7    8


     D E N E N B E C H E R W E R F
     1   1       1   1 1   1
     3 4 1 5 2 1 6 2 0 7 3 5 8 4 9

          First Key for 9 August


     E C H E R W E R F D E N E N B
     1   1 1 1   1       1   1
     4 2 0 5 3 5 8 4 9 3 7 1 8 2 1

          Second Key for 9 August
```

Fig. 5. Double transposition: Berlin-Teheran

Double Transposition/Substitution

Three systems involving both double transposition and substitution were introduced in the summer of 1943 after Chief Inspector Fritz Menzer of the Cipher Department of the German Army High Command was given the job of revamping all clandestine cryptosystems.

The first to appear was the "ABC Key" (see figure 6) which appeared on all Hamburg-controlled

```
P      : A B C D E F G H I J K L M N O P Q R S T U V W X Y Z

C      I: A N W B K V E G S H C P Y I D Q Z L J T M F R U O X
      II:                   I Y D Q           U R O X
     III:                   D I Y Q           O U R X
      IV:                   Q I O Y           X U O R
```

Substitution alphabets
Keyword Transposition mixed sequence using keyword HIMMELBLAU (sky blue)

```
K R A F T W A G E N F U E H R E R S C H E I N P R U E F U N G
1 2     2 3   1   1 1 2   1 2     2 2   1   1 1 2 2 2   1 3 2 1
7 2 1 9 7 1 2 2 4 8 0 8 5 4 3 8 4 6 3 5 7 6 9 1 6 9 8 1 0 0 3

* * * * * * * * D E I N E N R V I E R X X W A S C H B E R I
C H T E T O L D S M O B I L E X O L D S M O B I L E H E R S T
E L L T M O N A T L I C H H U N D E R T T A U S E N D S T U E
C K E I N S F U E N F F U E N F M M X M M U N D H U N D E R T
T A U S E N D S T U E C K E I N S N U L L F U E N F M M X M M
```

First transposition rectangle

```
* * * * * * * * B R G Y R Y Z M G R Z U U F A L W E B R Z G
W E J U J Y C 8 L P Y N G C U R Y C B L P Y N G C U E U Z L J
O C C J P I D A J C G W E E T D B O Z J J A T L O D B L J T O
W S X G O L K T X Q K K T X Q K P P U P P T Q B E T Q B X Z J
J A T L R Y B L J T R W H R G Y L Y T C C K T R Y K P P U P P
```

Substitution

```
* * * * * * * * J C * X T C D K B R B Z U T L J X J Y G E T H Z
R D K Y U P J P C * E E B Q P U J G L R Y G K R B U L B P B A
T L G J O J P R C * E X R Z L J P C U Y A T K W O W J B P C Q
T F N T Q T Z L T * Z P A G L B R E C S A Y U T Q G M Y B P L
L C O E Y G C O P * Y J P Q R G N W K W W U D T K R Z J X U O
O S N
```

Second transposition rectangle

Transposition rectangles for December 18 (12/18). Text is inscribed horizontally into the first rectangle, substitution is made; the resulting text is inscribed horizontally into the second rectangle, and extracted according to the ABC key.

Fig. 6

circuits in Europe and Africa. The system used double columnar transposition and monoalphabetic substitution with variants. The substitution cipher alphabet was a keyword transposition mixed sequence and was applied after the message was written into the first transposition rectangle. The variants were introduced by placing the letter *E* between *W* and *X* in the plain component for German-language messages and the letter *A* between *V* and *W* in Spanish-language messages. These alphabets were used without change in the first, fifth, and ninth lines of the first transposition rectangle. Figure 6 shows how the cipher component was changed for the second, sixth, and tenth lines; the third, seventh, and eleventh lines; and the fourth, eighth, and twelfth lines.

The transposition key was 31-long, usually an easily remembered phrase or compound word. In the first rectangle, all first row squares to the left of the column whose key number was the same as the date of encipherment were blocked out and the plain text started in that column. In the second rectangle, the column corresponding to the date and all first row squares to the left of the column corresponding to the month were blocked out, and the text was started in the latter column. If the two numbers were the same, then the column was not blocked out in the second rectangle, and both rectangles were the same. Figure 6 also shows two rectangles prepared for the substitution and transposition.

The major weakness of the system was that once a message was completely solved, all traffic enciphered on the same basic phrase was readable and keys remained in effect for three to six months.

At about the same time that the ABC Key was introduced on the Hamburg circuits, other forms of combined double transposition and substitution were introduced on the Berlin-controlled circuits. Descriptions of only two of these, Procedure 62 and Procedure 40, are available.

Procedure 62 used a 31-long key in which the key phrase was written out in two lines. The first line of sixteen characters had a space after each letter, with the spaces numbered from 1 to 15. The second line was started in the space corresponding to the number of the month of encryption and wrapped around. The following illustrates the procedure, using the phrase LA MUJER MAS HERMOSA EN ESPANA DEL SUR for the month of April.

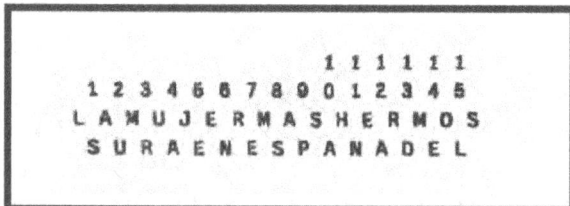

```
                      1 1 1 1 1
      1 2 3 4 5 6 7 8 9 0 1 2 3 4 5
      L A M U J E R M A S H E R M O S
      S U R A E N E S P A N A D E L
```

The two lines were then merged

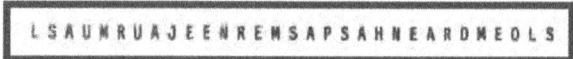

```
L S A U M R U A J E E N R E M S A P S A H N E A R D M E O L S
```

and the numerical key derived in the usual manner.

In the first transposition rectangle, the column immediately to the left of the number corresponding to the date was blocked out, as were all squares to the left of this column on the first line. In the second rectangle the column was not blocked out, but the same first row squares were. A trivial substitution was applied to the text in the first rectangle to camouflage the letters *A* and *E*.

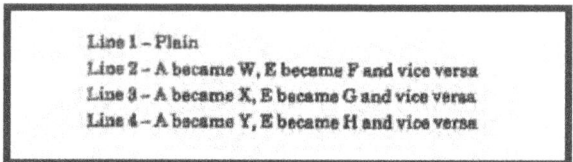

```
Line 1 – Plain
Line 2 – A became W, E became F and vice versa
Line 3 – A became X, E became G and vice versa
Line 4 – A became Y, E became H and vice versa
```

This four-line cycle was repeated throughout the message.

Procedure 40 was used on the Madrid-Ceuta circuit as a back-up system to the cipher machine normally used. In this procedure substitution took place before the first transposition. Both transposition and substitution used the same key phrase.

For substitution, a keyword mixed sequence derived from the key phrase, in this example DONDE MENOS SEPIENSA SALTA LA LIEBRA, was written into a 5x5 square omiting the letter *J*.

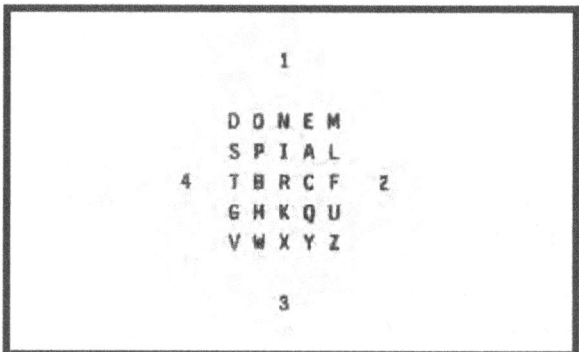

```
                    1

            D O N E M
            S P I A L
        4   T B R C F   2
            G H K Q U
            V W X Y Z

                    3
```

The plain text was divided into five-letter groups and the following substitution was made group by group:

The first letter was replaced by the letter above it in the square.
The second letter was replaced by the letter to its right in the square.
The third letter was replaced by the letter below it in the square.
The fourth letter was replaced by the letter to its left in the square.
The fifth letter was left plain.

The letter *J* was left plain in all positions. Thus, MESSAGE would become ZMTLA TM....

In the first transposition rectangle all squares in the first line to the left of the number corresponding to the date of encipherment were blocked out. In the second rectangle, the same was done to the first line squares to the left of the number corresponding to the month of encipherment.

The Kryha Machine

The Kryha machine was a clockwork-powered mechanical running key encipherment device. Two alphabets were on movable tabs so that the sequences of the plain component and the cipher component could be changed at will. The movement of the cipher alphabet disk was controlled by a cogwheel with sixty-two holes around the edge. A plunger on the end of a lever served as a detent by dropping into each of the holes in succession. These holes could be individually covered, thus changing the wheel pattern, and varying the "kick" with each step of the wheel. The total kick in one full revolution was prime to 26 so that the period of the machine was equal to 26 times the total kick. The cryptovariables of the system were therefore the plain sequence, the cipher sequence, the wheel pattern, the initial setting of the cogwheel, and the initial setting of the cipher sequence against the plain sequence. The last two variables were changed with each message, the others less frequently.

A pair of indicators, enciphered with a multivalued number key gave the alphabet setting (the number of the cipher letter set against *O* plain) in the "ab" positions, and the cogwheel setting in the "de" positions. The "c" position was a filler.

The clockwork-driven Kryha, a popular German-made cipher machine that was widely used commercially in the 1930s

The Menzer Device

When Chief Inspector Menzer had been tasked by Admiral Canaris with testing the security of the Abwehr cryptosystems in 1942, he found them depressingly inadequate. In addition to the ABC Key, Procedure 40, and Procedure 62, he introduced the cipher plate and the cipher wheel as field agent cipher devices, and Cipher Device 41 for use by Abwehr nets within Germany.[1]

line opposite the plain value would be read, and the cipher value taken from the cell with that number.[2]

The cipher wheel was another hand-operated cipher device designed for agent use. It was made up of two disks mounted concentrically. The lower disk had fifty-two notches or holes around its edge into which a pencil or stylus could be inserted to turn the disk. On the face of the disk were fifty-two cells into which a keyword-mixed alphabet

Menzer device

The cipher plate was designed by Menzer specifically for agent use. It consisted of a circular box about the size of a shoe polish can containing three resettable notched wheels and a spring. On the top a mixed alphabet could be written with pencil or grease pencil, thirteen characters on the fixed ring and thirteen on the moveable ring. The disk was rotated to wind the spring for encipherment. Pressing a button on the side would release the disk and allow it to rotate until stopped by the notch rings. If the disk stopped in a position where its letters were in phase with those on the outer ring, the cipher value was read directly. If the stop was in an intermediate position, the number of the

could be inscribed twice, clockwise. The upper disk had a direct standard alphabet inscribed on half of its periphery, next to a semicircular window that revealed twenty-six characters of the mixed sequence on the lower disk. The upper disk also had a notch cut into its edge which exposed ten of the holes on the lower disk. This notch had the numbers 0 to 9 inscribed next to it, in a counterclockwise direction, so that when the exposed holes were lined up with the numbers, the letters on the lower disk were lined up with the letters on the upper disk.

Various methods of key generation were used. On Chilean circuits an eleven-letter key word was numbered as for a transposition key, with the first digit of two-digit numbers dropped. The key was extended by appending a two-digit group count and a four-digit time group:

ANTOFOGASTA
1 6 074 8 5 2913121440

On other circuits a Fibonacci sequence of 100-125 digits would be generated through various manipulations of the date, time, and agent number. If the message was longer than the key, the latter would be reversed as many times as necessary. Key generation tables were also used.

The key constituted the input to an autoclave. After the alphabets were aligned according to an indicator in the message, a stylus was inserted in the hole corresponding to the first key digit, and the lower disk was rotated clockwise until the stylus was stopped by the end of the notch. The plaintext letter was then found on the upper disk, and its cipher value was read off of the lower disk. The stylus was then placed in the hole, corresponding to the second digit of key, and the same procedure was repeated for the second letter of text. Thus the true key at any point in the cipher was equal to the sum of all the previous key inputs.[3]

The Cipher Device 41 was a cipher machine invented by Menzer in 1941 which was based on

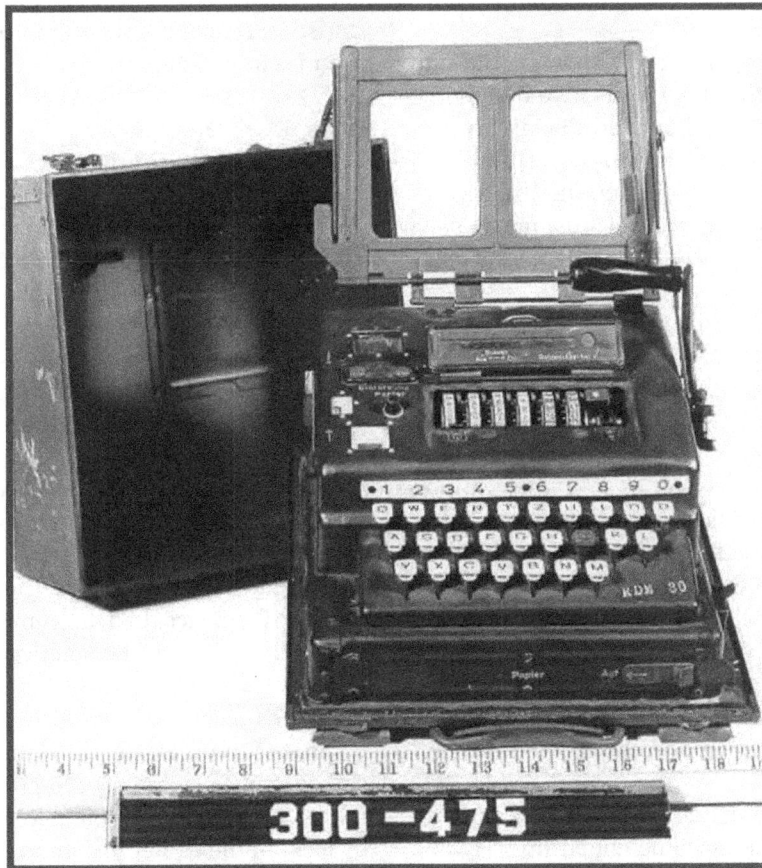

Menzer Device SG-41–A successful encipherment system,
but of limited use due to its heavy weight

Hagelin encipherment but included a mechanism for variably stepping the Hagelin wheels. The Cipher Device 41 had six pin wheels that were mutually prime. The first five wheels had kicks of 1, 2, 4, 8, and 10, respectively; the sixth wheel made these kicks positive or negative. The enciphering cycle (encipherment of one letter) consisted of three elements:

1. This took place if and only if the sixth key wheel had an active pin in the "motion index position." If this were the case, then all of the following occurred: Wheel 1 moved one step, and each of the remaining four wheels moved one step unless the wheel to its left had an active pin in the "motion index position," in which case it would move two steps.

2. A key kick was generated which was the sum of the kicks of wheels which had active pins in the "kick index position." If, however, the sixth wheel had an active pin in the "kick index position," the key kick would be twenty-five minus the sum of all of the other kicks. In other words, under such a circumstance, the key would complement itself.

3. This was identical to Step 1, except that it occurred whether or not Wheel 6 had an active pin in the "motion index position." In this step, Wheel 6 also stepped one or two positions, depending on the state of Wheel 5.

The original specifications called for a lightweight, durable machine to be used by military units forward of division. Menzer designed it to provide a cipher tape and to be keyboard-operated to improve the speed of encipherment. As a result of the keyboard operation, he was able to redesign the arrangement of letters on the print wheels to flatten the cipher frequency count.[4]

Because of the wartime shortages of aluminum and magnesium, the machine ended up weighing between twelve and fifteen kilograms, too heavy for field use. Removal of the keyboard would have lightened the machine, but the redesign of the

print wheels prevented their being used directly for encipherment. Production stopped because no one knew what to do. About 1,000 machines had been constructed and were distributed to the Abwehr which began using them on circuits within Europe in 1944.[5]

GC&CS read a number of Cipher Device 41 messages through depth reading techniques, but even after some of the machines had been captured and examined, no one could postulate a theory of cryptanalytic attack. A 1947 WDGAS-71 report stated that if a mechanically reliable machine could be built embodying the same principles as the Cipher Device 41, it would undoubtedly be a valuable asset. The report noted that because of the key complementing characteristic of the machine, statistical tests did not seem to offer any particular promise for solution.[6]

The Coast Guard Solution of Enigma: The Commercial Machine

In January 1940 Coast Guard intercept operators collected a suspicious circuit using the calls MAN V NDR, RDA V MAN, and the like, transmitting one to five encrypted messages a day. It soon became apparent that all messages intercepted were in flush depth, although the method of encipherment was as yet unknown.

Attempts to solve the first twenty or thirty messages in depth met with no success because of badly garbled copy and lack of any definite evidence as to the underlying language. By the time sixty or seventy messages had accumulated, however, it seemed certain that the language was German and that a word separator had been used.

In the progressive development of the plain cipher equivalences for each position of the depth, it was observed that no plain letter was represented by itself in the cipher text and that the plain cipher equivalences within each alphabet were reciprocal. This, together with the language, seemed ample justification for assuming that the traffic had been encrypted on an Enigma cipher machine. The Coast Guard Intelligence Unit had a model of the commercial version of the machine together with the original manufacturer's instructions and suggestions for its use. These instructions included the practice of using "X" as a word separator, and of representing numbers by their equivalent letters as shown on the keyboard of the machine:

1 2 3 4 5 6 7 8 9 0
Q W E R T Z U I O P

After almost fully recovering the first thirty-two alphabets, the Coast Guard cryptanalysts developed a technique for stripping off the effect of the reflector and then of successive wheels, resulting in a complete solution of the machine with all wirings. The wiring recovered in this solution later proved to be known wiring, but the Coast Guard recovery of wiring assumed to be unknown was achieved without prior knowledge of any solution or technique. This is believed to be the first instance of

Enigma wiring recovery in the United States. It should be noted that the initial approach to the problem was an adaptation of the procedure used in the solution of the Hebern machine.

From the equivalent wirings of the two outside wheels, the Signal Intelligence Service (SIS) identified them as the actual ones furnished in the old commercial Enigma machine, and the Navy later identified the traffic as Swiss army. With respect to the numbers on the actual wheels, the wheel order used was 1-3-2 (left to right, as one faced the machine).

The Coast Guard Solution of Enigma: The Green Machine[7]

A station using the call TQI2 was first heard on 10 October 1942 on 10,415 kHz. The station sent calls only up to 30 October, when a message was intercepted. The message preamble was 2910/301/66. TQI2 was believed to be linked with

Enigma with extra rotors

a station using the call TIM2 on 11,310 kHz. On 12 November 1942, it was learned from bearings taken by the FCC that TQI2 was in Europe and TIM2 was in South America. This was confirmed by the Radio Security Service (RSS) at a radio intelligence meeting on 17 November on the basis of Hamburg-Bordeaux traffic which was being read by GC&CS. The Bordeaux terminal had been instructed to monitor the circuit and to assist in case of difficulty. Station TQI2 also used the call RSE, which was believed to be the alternate control in Bordeaux.

During October and December 1942, twenty-eight messages were intercepted from TQI2. This series of messages had several duplicate message numbers (two 315s, three 316s, etc.) The messages were tested for depth and, although the coincidence rate was definitely above random, it was rather poor. It was assumed, therefore, that most of the messages were encrypted on the same key, but that the duplicate message numbers were possible evidence of different keys. Actually, all messages turned out to have been encrypted on the same key. The poor coincidence rate was a result of the inclusion of several practice messages in the series. These practice messages contained a short text at the beginning and were filled out to average length with dummy text.

The lessons learned from solving the commercial Enigma were applied, together with the improved techniques learned from the British, and the machine was solved. Wheel motion patterns were similar to the Enigmas used by German agents in Europe which had been solved by the British prior to the appearance of TQI2. Decrypted texts showed that the circuit was between Berlin and Argentina.

On 11 January 1943 messages were transmitted with external serial numbers 322-328. It was possible to align these in depth by stepping each successive message one position to the right, producing a ten-letter repeat in messages 322 and 327. The complete plain text was quickly reconstructed. Two later sets of messages sent in June and July confirmed the method used on this circuit for determining monthly ring settings and normal positions.

The Coast Guard Solution of Enigma: The Red Machine

The first mention of this machine appeared in message number 145 from Argentina to Berlin on 4 November 1943. This message was sent on the "Green" circuit and encrypted on the "Green" Enigma. The message read

THE TRUNK TRANSMITTER WITH ACCESSORIES AND ENIGMA ARRIVED VIA RED. THANK YOU VERY MUCH. FROM OUR MESSAGE 150 WE SHALL ENCIPHER WITH THE NEW ENIGMA. WE SHALL GIVE THE OLD DEVICE TO GREEN. PLEASE ACKNOWLEDGE BY RETURN MESSAGE WITH NEW ENIGMA.

[s] LUNA

On the same day, the "Red" section sent message number 989 stating that an additional Enigma machine had arrived. This message had been encrypted with the Kryha machine which the Coast Guard had solved.

On 5 November 1943, Berlin sent message number 585 to the "Green" section in Argentina:

RE YOUR 145: NEW ENIGMA IS INTENDED FOR RED ONLY.

The following day, Berlin sent message number 917 to the "Red" section:

INTERN 86. THE NEW ENIGMA WHICH ARRIVED TOGETHER WITH TRUNK TRANSMITTER IS FOR RED. IT IS A BIRTHDAY SURPRISE FOR LUNA.

On the same day, 6 November, the "Red" section in Argentina sent message number 991 requesting a key for the new Enigma, asking that it be sent via the "Blue" key (unsolved) and not via the "Red" Kryha key. The message went on to say that they were constantly making a fundamental blunder in transmitting a new key by means of the old one.

Berlin replied to this message on 9 November, asking the "Red" section to be patient for a few more days until a key for the new Enigma could be forwarded.

At this point there ensued a considerable amount of confusion regarding methods of transmission of key, settings for the "Red" Enigma, and settings for the "Red" Kryha, all of which was finally resolved by 14 December. Once the Germans got their encryption procedures squared away, the Coast Guard solved the "Red" Enigma by normal methods.

The Coast Guard Solution of Enigma: The Berlin-Madrid Machine

About 5 May 1944, the Berlin-Madrid circuit stopped using double transposition and began using Enigma. An examination of the traffic on a single day revealed that messages from the same transmitting agent could be superimposed in depth by use of the time group. For example, a message having a preamble encipherment time of 1410 would be in phase with a message encrypted at 1400 hours from the eleventh letter of the latter message. This was similar to one method previously encountered on the Berlin-Argentina circuit, where a secret daily-changing number was added to the encryption time and the machine was then stepped that number of positions forward from the basic key for the day.

After determining the indicator system being used, the various Enigmas used by the Security Service group, of which the Berlin-Madrid circuit was a part, were considered. Only four machines had been employed by this group: the "Green," the "Red," a combination of "Red" wheels and a "Green" reflector, and the so-called "M" machine. Assuming that the traffic was encrypted on one of the known machines, a considerable time was expended on guesses in depth (the depth of any series of messages was never enough to yield a solution by that method alone) followed by running menus on the sliding GRENADE and checking the resulting hits in the uncribbed depth.

This method eventually read the system on a depth of twelve. The successful cribs were easily expanded and the full text recovered. The machine involved employed the "Red" wheels and the "Green" reflector. The only other time this type of usage was encountered was when the instructions for the "Red" machine were first sent to Argentina.

The Coast Guard Solution of Enigma: The Hamburg-Bordeaux Stecker

In the period immediately preceding the change from hand to machine system, several Hamburg-Bordeaux messages were solved which proved to be reencipherments of unidentified cipher texts. These had a short plaintext internal preamble giving a serial number, letter count, and a cover name to identify the encrypted traffic.

An analysis of the plain texts of messages encrypted in the old system showed that some type of radio intercept activity was involved. From this information it was deduced that the Bordeaux end of the circuit acted as a sort of monitoring and relay station which listened in to certain outstations for the Hamburg control and furnished Hamburg with the texts of outstation messages which Hamburg had failed to receive.

Further information was secured through a reencryption sent by Bordeaux. Ten groups of a message were sent; the transmission was interrupted and later a message was sent which repeated the ten groups with some of the letters changed. The changed letters had been substituted in a manner which suggested that a stecker had been employed and that one or perhaps two wires had been improperly plugged. The combination of the stecker and the three-letter indicator found on the traffic strongly suggested the use of the German Service wheels.

The next step in the analysis was the identification of the traffic reencrypted in the last days of the old hand system. This proved to be traffic from the FBI-controlled Hamburg-New York circuit. By examining message lengths and transmission times, it was then possible to find days on which Bordeaux had reencrypted New York traffic by machine and relayed it to Hamburg. Correct message placement supplied cribs which were tried on the Bombe and the machine was solved. It proved to be using Service wheels 1, 2, and 3 with a fixed "Bruno" reflector and adapter.

From a security standpoint, the conditions under which this circuit operated exhibited an almost complete abandonment of good cryptographic practices. Not only did the Germans use their most secure cryptomachine to retransmit low-grade traffic, but the settings used were those employed on Spanish Abwehr nets. Furthermore, there were indications that the Germans were aware that the New York circuit was controlled – yet the reencryption of this low-grade traffic was permitted. This was also the only example known to the Coast Guard of the Service machine being employed for clandestine traffic.

The British Effort

Clandestine traffic worked by the British fell into three cryptographic segments called ISK (Illicit Series Knox), ISOS (Illicit Services Oliver Strachey) and ISTUN (Illicit Series TUNNY). Two sections at Bletchley Park were solely engaged on clandestine: Section ISK was wholly cryptanalytic, and Section ISOS did crypt work on all traffic other than ISK and ISTUN. ISOS also was the intelligence and distributing center for the entire clandestine output. ISTUN was broken by the TUNNY Section under Pritchard which handled all TUNNY traffic including clandestine.[8]

Bletchley Park

The Bombe, named for the loud ticking sound it made during operation

As of mid-1943, the ISK Section had the use of one to two Bombes, but most of the work was done by hand, and the Bombes were used only for research and particularly difficult keys. The solutions were entirely based on probable word and cribs were frequently derived from ISOS traffic. The solution of a key usually took one to three days, but was often much faster if demanded, as in the case of Spanish traffic during the Mediterranean operations.[9]

The traffic intake was about 350 messages per day, of which about 300 were read. Much of the unreadable traffic was too garbled; the Norwegian keys were especially difficult. Spanish Morocco used the commercial type Enigma, but all the other ISK machines were uniform except the Paris-Canaries circuit, which had its own wiring. ISK was used mostly by important Abwehr stations in RSS groups II, XIII, XIV, and VII/23. It was estimated

that the coverage of Spanish ISK was 95 percent complete, Balkans 75 percent, Berlin to Turkey 80 percent, and 90 percent for group VII/23. After the messages were broken, they were sent to the ISOS Section for translating and distribution.

The ISK machine was introduced at the end of 1940 and was first broken by the British on Christmas Day, 1941.[10]

The ISOS Section was established at the end of 1939 and by mid-1943 was reading about 150 illicit radio circuits. The traffic consisted of a wide variety of transposition and substitution ciphers, with the traffic usually in German but including considerable Spanish and French and occasionally many other languages. All RSS groups, except VIII, XII, XIV, and XVI carried only Abwehr traffic. Groups VIII and XVI were Italian Secret Intelligence and were not handled by ISOS but by Bletchley Park's

TUNNY

Research Section. Group XIII was ISK and ISOS traffic of the Security Service; Group XIV carried Abwehr traffic, both ISK and ISOS and diplomatic traffic. Group XIII ISOS traffic was double transposition. Groups I and XV used simple transposition; Group XIV ISOS, included a variety of substitution and double transposition.[11]

In 1943 the average daily ISOS traffic intake was 150-200 messages per day. All incoming traffic was sorted in the ISOS Section Registry Room into RSS groups and sent to the appropriate sections, all three of which sent their decodes back to the ISOS Registry Room, which handed decodes to the Watch Room. The Watch Room ran twenty-four hours, with eight people usually on duty except on the graveyard shift when there was only one. The Watch Room translated and amended the texts, which were often severely garbled. Messages then went to typists who made sixteen English copies and also German copies for certain users. The Watch Room kept a file of recent back traffic in German, and the Registry Room kept a complete back file in English. As of June 1943, GC&CS had produced 115,000 clandestine serial numbers, of which a little over half were ISOS type. One serial number frequently contained one or several messages, averaging about two per serial number.

During 1942 GC&CS produced 61,267 serial numbers, and the daily average rose from 101 to 209. ISOS, ISK, and ISTUN were circulated twice daily (each in a separate series) to MI6, to the three service ministries, to MI5 and RSS. Group XIII was circulated separately twice daily, under the title "ISOSICLE," to the same recipients, plus the London Office of the Chief of the Secret Service. In addition, the following special series were circulated:

1. ISMEW traffic from the Bilbao-Biarritz circuit, covering the movements of ore boats, went to MEW in addition to usual customers;

2. ISBA, containing all messages referring to British agents abroad, went only to MI-6;

3. TUNNY traffic, referring to DF of British transmitters, went only to MI-8;

4. Paris to Stuttgart traffic, referring to White Russians who listened in on Paris to Russian radio telephone conversations, was circulated only to the office of CSS;

5. Norwegian traffic went to the usual customers; and

6. The Intelligence Branch of ISOS kept indexes of persons and places; studied organization of the Abwehr and Security Service, abbreviations, vocabulary, and cover names. It studied ISOS for cribs into ISK and both for cribs into Enigma or other traffic. It maintained liaison with the recipients of the output and studied the entire output for the benefit of the section as a whole.[12]

In 1943 most of the ISOS traffic was in Groups II and VII, with a considerable amount in Group I, and a little in Group III. The principal topics of the messages were[13]

1. Chetnik and Partisan operations in Yugoslavia;

2. Naval observations from Spain and Portugal of Iberian harbors, Gibraltar, and the Eastern Mediterranean;

3. Agents reports from Spanish Morocco on the situation in North Africa;

4. Military developments in Turkey and the Near East, including disposition of Turkish forces and arrivals of British missions;

5. Red Cross activities in Greece;

6. Ship movements in the North Sea and of the Scandinavian coast;

7. Military intelligence about Russian troop movements;

8. General arrangements for carrying on espionage;

9. Slipping agents through to their destination;

10. Administrative;

11. Service messages on radio communications and use of ciphers.

Almost all ISK traffic was in Groups II and XIV and occasionally Group VII. The principal subjects were[14]

1. Naval observations from Spain and Spanish Morocco;

2. Administrative;

3. Naval observations in the Near East;

4. British troop movements in the Near East;

5. Military activity in Turkey;

6. Naval activity in the Black Sea;

7. Partisan and Chetnik warfare in Yugoslavia;

8. Organization of communists in Yugoslavia;

9. Slipping agents into Turkey;

10. Russian military movements;

11. Conditions in Iran;

12. Military supplies from the Allies to Turkey;

13. Inquiries about the loyalty and reliability of individuals.

ISTUN traffic was not intercepted by RSS but by the non-Morse intercept station at Knockholt and, therefore, did not carry RSS group numbers but was entirely Abwehr traffic. The great bulk of the messages was between Berlin and Greece and included much information on suspected individuals, some messages on German propaganda to Arab countries, and a little on enterprises of Branch 11.[15]

ISOSICLE messages were transmitted between Berlin and Lisbon, Istanbul, Sofia, Madrid, Bucharest, Helsinki, Switzerland, Budapest, Tetuan, Paris, Marseilles, and unknown locations. This was traffic of the Security Service, and was very different from Abwehr traffic, much more diplomatic and political. The principal topics were[16]

1. The Finnish political situation;

2. Finnish broadcasts to Estonia embarrassing to the Germans because of "underlying democratic ideology" and because the Germans had forbidden the Estonians to listen to foreign radio;

3. Italian activities in Corsica, which seemed to foreshadow Italian attempt at colonization and annexation;

4. Jewish problem in Bulgaria;

5. The troubles of the American army in Algiers;

6. Economic warfare plans;

7. Administrative;

8. Communications service.

The reliability of information contained in Abwehr and Security Service traffic varied widely, from completely inaccurate to substantially accurate. Intelligence reports were often prepared by paid agents and had to be assessed in that light.[17]

Notes

1. 79/49/TOPSEC/AS-14, TICOM DF.174, "Description of Contacts of Fritz Menzer with American and Soviet Authorities and Summary of Career," 21.

2. 79/49/TOPSEC/AS-14, 33: and 33/51/TOPSEC/AFSA-14, R-2, "Schlueuelscheibe 50" (May 1951).

3. LCDR L.A. Griffiths, RNVR, GC&CS Secret Service SIGINT, Vol. III, 111-15.

4. WDGAS-14's European Axis Signal Intelligence in World War II as Revealed by TICOM Investigations and Other Prisoner of War Interrogations and Captured Material, Principally German, Vol. II, 29.

5. Ibid., 29.

6. TICOM DF-19, "Cipher Device-41" (10 January 1944); Memorandum from Frank W. Lewis, WDGAS-71, to COL Solomon Kullback, WDGAS-70, "Study of the C-41 Cipher Device" (4 March 1947), and GC&CS Secret Service SIGINT, Vol. II, 166-171.

7. The descriptives "Red" and "Green" were applied by traffic analysts to Enigma to designate different circuits serving two different groups of agents. In addition, the setups on the two machines differed.

8. COL Alfred McCormack's report on his trip to London, May-June 1943, 42. 9. Ibid., 42-43.

10. Ibid., 43.

11. Ibid., 44-45.

12. Ibid., 44-47.

13. Ibid., 47-48.

14. Ibid., 48-49.

15. Ibid., 49.

16. Ibid., 49-50.

17. Ibid., 50

Glossary
(Applies to Parts I and II)

Abteilung	Branch
Abwehr	Counterintelligence
Abwehrleitstelle (A1st)	Counterintelligence Control Post
Abwehrstelle (Ast)	Counterintelligence Post
Allgemeine SS	General SS
Amt	Department
Grundstellung	Setting
Gruppe	Group
Hauptabteilung	Bureau
Krieporganization (KO)	Combat Organization
Meldekopf (MK)	Message Center
Nebenstelle (Nest or Anst)	Branch Post
Oberinspektor	Chief Inspector
Oberkommando Wehrmacht (OKW)	High Command of the Armed Forces
Oberkommando des Heeres	Army High Command
Reich	The nation
Reichsfuehrer	Leader of the Reich
Reichssicherheitshauptamt (RSHA)	Reich Security Administration
Schluesselgeraet	Crypto Device
Schluesselrad	Cipher Wheel

Schluesselscheibe	Cipher Plate
Schutzstaffel (SS)	The SS, Blackshirts (lit., "Protection Squad")
Sicherheitsdienst (SD)	Security Service
Sicherheitspolizei (SiPo)	Security Police
Sondeschluessel	Probe Key
Unternehmen	(Special) Operations
Verfahren	Procedure
Wehrkreis	Military District
Zahlschluessel	Key Number

This publication is dedicated to the memory of David P. Mowry, one of NSA's longest serving employees.

Dave also researched and wrote numerous histories, including the booklets German Cipher Machines of World War II *and* Listening to the Rumrunners *(two of the pamphlets most in demand at the National Cryptologic Museum). An expert cryptanalyst, he studied under the legendary Lambros Callimahos and served many years as a senior linguist in operations. His assignments included a variety of NSA locations in the United States and overseas. Late in life he learned how to work magic on computers, and his initiatives made the first CCH webpage on NSAnet a truly user-friendly site. He also displayed historical cryptologic equipment (such as the Enigma machine) to both the NSA workforce and the general public at numerous Agency-sponsored events. Finally, one of his last contributions to the CCH was as co-author of the history on SIGINT controversies related to the Pearl Harbor attack—a monograph that will become required reading for all future historians writing about the "Day of Infamy."*